TWO-END KNITTING

by

Anne-Maj Ling

A Traditional Scandinavian Technique

(also known as "Twined Knitting")

From Basics to New Refinements & Designs

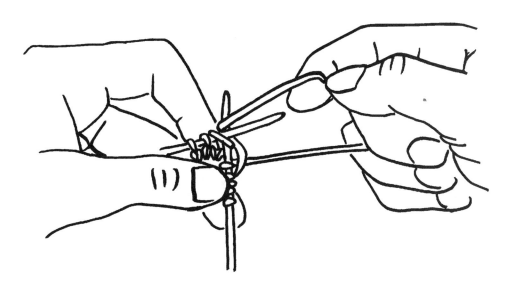

Text and Photos: Anne-Maj Ling

Drawings: Gunvor Eriksson

English Translation: Carol Huebscher Rhoades

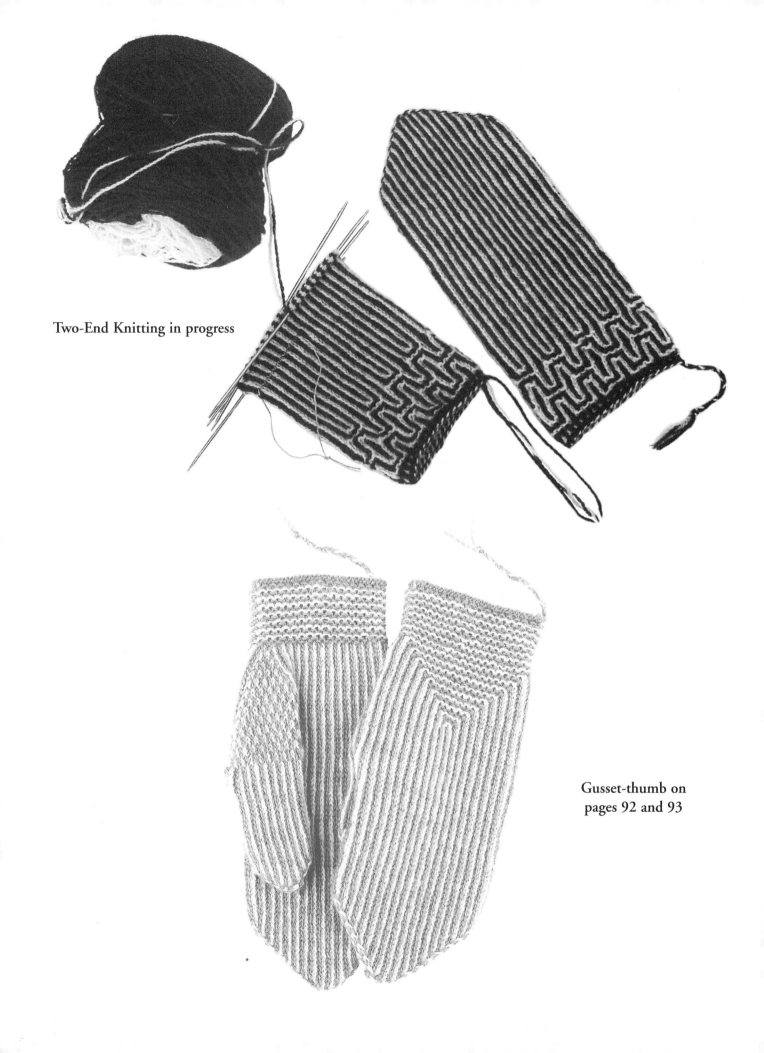

Two-End Knitting in progress

Gusset-thumb on
pages 92 and 93

TWO-END KNITTING

Originally printed in Sweden by Firma Krokmaskan - 2002

English translation by Carol Huebscher Rhoades and Anne-Maj Ling - 2003

First English printing by Schoolhouse Press - 2004
Second Schoolhouse Press printing, 2007

Library of Congress Control Number 2003114321

ISBN #978-0-942018-23-3

Schoolhouse Press
6899 Cary Bluff
Pittsville, WI 54466
(715) 884-2799
www.schoolhousepress.com

Mitten with gusset-thumb: page 90 & 91

Mitten with straight-thumb: page 74 & 76

Stockings on page 96.

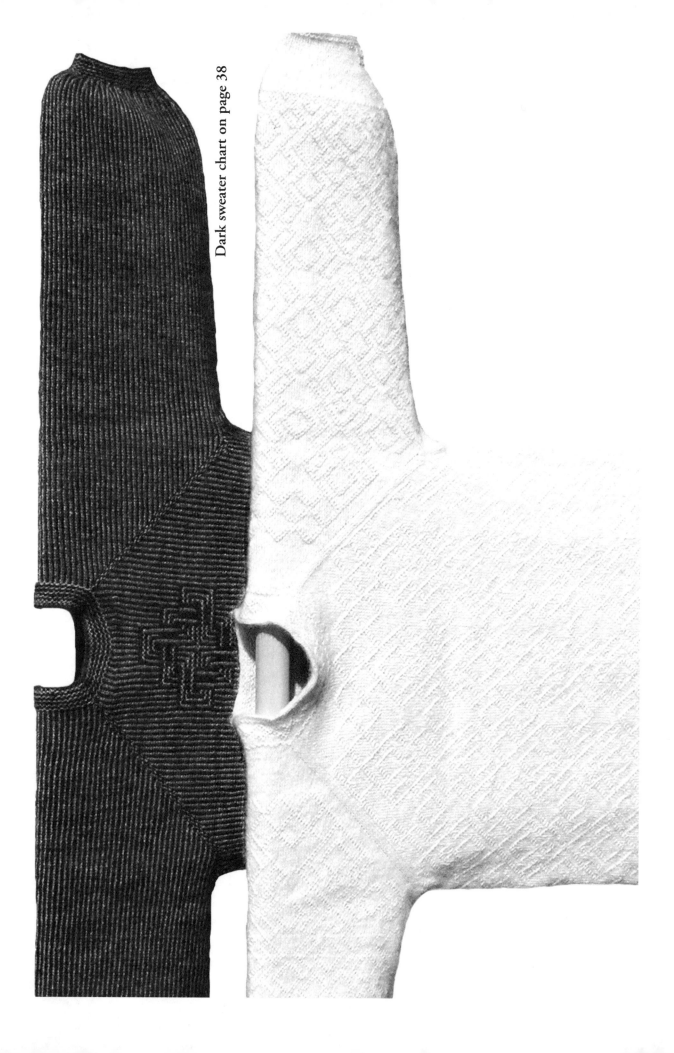

Dark sweater chart on page 38

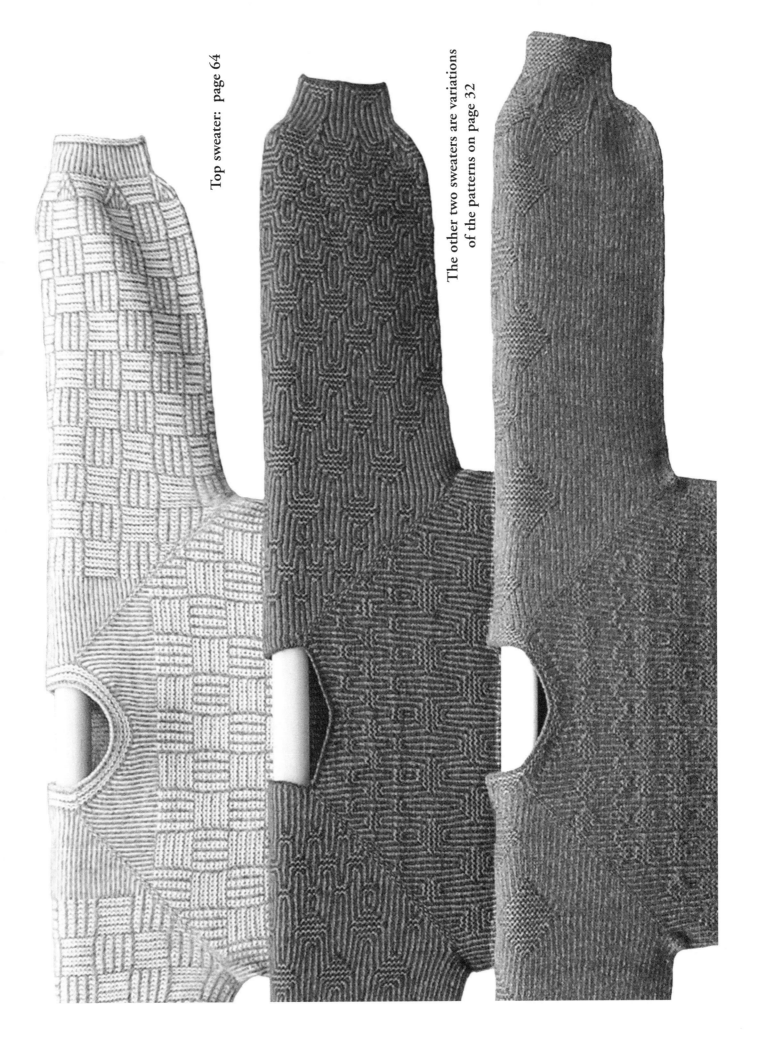

Top sweater: page 64

The other two sweaters are variations
of the patterns on page 32

Knitted Dickey: see page 68

Knitted skirts, L to R: see page 72, 71, 73

The border pattern chart for this skirt is on page 37; second from the left

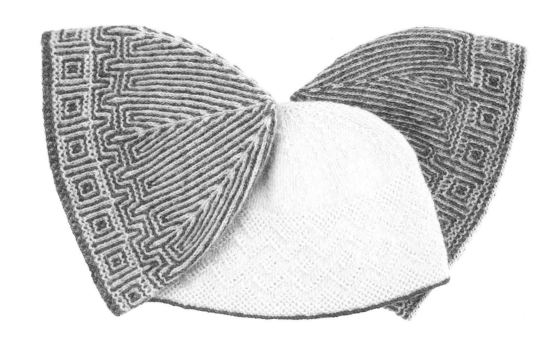

For the construction of these hats, see page 97.
The two-color motifs are variations of the chart on page 32

Clockwise from upper L: page 97, page 99 (chart on page 32),
page 99 (chart on page 37- 3rd from L), page 97, page 97

TABLE OF CONTENTS

FOREWORD

Two-end knitting is a unique Scandinavian knitting technique which is well worth preserving and developing. As the word two-end knitting suggests, one knits with two ends of the yarn and one knits "by throwing" in the old way. Both strands are held in the right hand and twisted around each other in the same direction between every stitch. This twisting gives a particularly firm yet flexible character to the finished garment.

At first glance, two-end knitting does not seem very different from regular knitting because the knit stitches look almost alike. If you look more closely, you will see that the stitches are a little skewed. On the wrong side, the difference is more apparent because the twist between the stitches makes rows of horizontal lines. The stitches so typical of two-end knitting and which form lovely surface patterns are called curled (*krus*) stitches and are made by alternating purl and knit stitches.

The technique was probably close to falling into extinction when an archeological find of a glove was made in Falun in 1974. Given the circumstances of the find, the glove can certainly be dated to before 1680. From the old records, we know that the slagheap under which the glove was found was in place then. The find awakened such a great interest that knowledge of the technique spread over the country and it can now be considered as rescued.

The techniques for working two-end knitting survived as knowledge handed down from mother to daughter, primarily in Dalarna and other forest landscapes of west Sweden. Well into the twentieth century, girls in those areas learned how to two-end knit in school handicraft classes. The most often knitted pieces were single-color mittens and stockings for men who worked in the forests but prettily patterned mittens were also made. Some could still knit the richly patterned sleeves for the sewn jacket bodices which are part of some parish costumes.

I learned the basics of two-end knitting from Kerstin Gustafsson in a course at Karlskoga folk high school in 1981. To begin with, I knitted mittens, caps, and stockings but thought a lot about how much I wanted to knit a whole sweater. The first attempt didn't work out but it showed that the project was feasible. The first sweater was finished in 1983.

As a student and friend of Mieko Yano from 1982 until her death, I gained valuable knowledge about regular knitting, some of which also proved useful for solving technical problems in two-end knitting. This knowledge has since helped me in the task of transforming two-end knitting techniques into garments with a style and color suitable for today's clothing. Over time, a great number of sweaters, jackets, skirts, and even a pair of trousers have come from my needles.

I continue to learn a great deal through the work of helping students in courses and study circles to realize the garments they want to knit. Questions need answers and, in order for an answer to be good, thought is needed which, in its turn, yields more knowledge and experience.

In the spring of 1986, I was accepted as a member of the Artisans Guild *(Konsthantverkarna)* in Stockholm. At the same time, I was invited to have an exhibition. It took a couple of years to knit enough material for the exhibit which I had in November, 1988. In the spring of 1988, I had an exhibit at the Dalarna Museum in Falun together with a group of students from South Närke which called itself "Ling's Journeymen."

In 1991, I published a handbook which I called "Aides for Two-End Knitting." I omitted the basics because the book *Tvåändsstickat* from LT's Publishing Company (English translation *Twined Knitting*, published by Interweave Press) was available in bookstores. That book is no longer in print, so I have revised my complete work and have added information on the basics.

With the hope that Gunvor and I have succeeded in conveying our knowledge in words and pictures, I wish you much benefit and enjoyment with two-end knitting.

Anne-Maj Ling

YARN

Wool Yarn

The choice of yarn is important for pleasant knitting and a good result. The yarn you choose will gain something in quality because, by being two-end knitted, it will have been worth the work. Z-plied wool yarn is easy to knit with; the garment will hold its shape; and the pattern will appear clearly.

Many who work with two-end knitting use regular S-plied wool yarn. That works quite well for mittens, stockings and other small pieces. It can also work well for larger garments if the plying isn't too tight. When one two-end knits with an S-plied yarn, the twist becomes tighter and tighter as one knits. Then, it becomes more difficult to control the strands of the yarn because they will twist on themselves and knot as the twist becomes tighter during the knitting. Even worse, the tightened twist can skew the garment. Make a good-sized swatch before you begin a large garment with S-plied yarn.

In contrast, Z-plied yarn becomes less twisted during the knitting. The yarn should be well-plied in order for it to be suitable for two-end knitting. If there is too little twist in the yarn, it can become totally untwisted and feel unpleasant. Those who spin their own yarn, should make a lightly twisted S-singles and a rather well-plied Z yarn.

A yarn suitable for two-end knitting should also be rather smooth, with the fibers parallel as in worsted yarn. This will make a large garment feel soft and pleasing and the pattern stitches will show up well. The technique is compact and, therefore, a light and lofty woolen yarn in which the fibers are at all angles, is not suitable. No matter how soft and fine such a yarn feels, it becomes prickly in a large two-end knitted garment.

Most of the wool yarns which are produced for handwork are unwashed if they are not dyed. If you handspin or buy unwashed yarn and will not dye it, you will get the best results if you also knit with the yarn unwashed.

Usually, yarns for handwork are not moth-proofed, so, don't let the yarn lie around for a long time without airing it in the sunshine occasionally. In addition, the finished garment should not lie undisturbed for long periods without being aired outside in order to prevent insect infestation. Keep wool, yarn, and wool garments in as cool a place as possible.

Other Yarns

Silk yarn is a surprisingly pleasant material for two-end knitting. It is pliant and easy to work with. The result is a stable, yet flexible material. Up to now, I've only tried two-ply schappe (fermentation degummed silk which is soft, supple, and lustrous) silk. It doesn't seem to matter if the silk yarn is S- or Z-plied, perhaps because the silk fibers are straight.

In earlier times, many lovely mittens were knitted with very fine linen or cotton yarn. A gauge of between 6 and 9 stitches per cm (15-22 stitches per inch) was obtained with needles 1.0 mm or 1.25 mm (U.S. sizes 00000 and 0000). I have only knitted some small swatches with the cotton yarn on the market now. The swatches showed that cabled cotton gives the best results. I have not yet tried linen yarn.

Synthetic and designer yarns gain nothing in either appearance or quality by being two-end knitted.

Sampler with S- and Z-plied Yarn

If you want to learn how the yarn performs depending on whether it is S- or Z-plied, you can two-end knit a sampler which is described in the book *Tvebinding* (Two-end Knitting) by Tove Frederiksen.

The sampler consists of 8 sections. The first 4 sections are knitted with Z-plied yarn and then the next 4 are knitted in the same way but with S-plied yarn. In order to get a true comparison, the yarns should be of the same quality.

Sections 1, 2, 5, and 6 are knitted with the regular European knit stitch: bring the yarn onto the needle from underneath as we normally do.

Sections 3, 4, 7, and 8 are knitted with the Asian knit stitch: bring the yarn down over the needle. On the next row, the needle must be inserted into the back of the stitch, otherwise the stitch will be what we call "a twisted stitch."

In every other section, the yarns are twisted around each other as normally – bring the back strand over the front strand.

For the alternate sections, the strands are twisted in the "wrong direction" – bring the back strand under the front one.

SECTION	YARN	STITCH	DIRECTION OF TWIST
1	Z	European	back strand over front
2	Z	European	back strand under front
3	Z	Asian	back strand over front
4	Z	Asian	back strand under front
5	S	European	back strand over front
6	S	European	back strand under front
7	S	Asian	back strand over front
8	S	Asian	back strand under front

If you want to have an example to see the difference between two-end knitting and regular knitting with two strands, you can finish the sampler with a ninth section:
Knit several rows with two strands without twisting them between the stitches (as you do for vertical stripes in regular knitting). The difference will be obvious when you see both ways of knitting on one sampler.

If you want to ascertain whether a yarn is S- or Z-plied, you can draw an S and a Z over a yarn. The direction of the letter's middle section is the same as the direction of the twist.

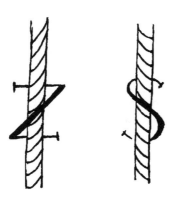

Opening up a Yarn Skein

In order to avoid tangles when you wind a skein of yarn, you need to be careful when you open up a skein. Be sure that all the strands lie in the same direction before you untie the knots. The yarn should not cross over the knotted ends.

Always begin winding from the skein in the same direction. It doesn't matter if you start from the beginning or the end of the skein, but it is important that you wind each skein in the same manner. If you unwind the skeins in different directions, it will be evident in a large garment by color shifts.

Winding the Yarn

As the name "two-end knitting" implies, you will knit with two ends of the yarn. Using a strand from each of two different balls of yarn will work but it is most practical to wind the balls so that you have two ends from one ball.

It is quickest to wind on a ball winder, but, if you don't have one, you can wind by hand onto a winding stick (*nystpinne*) or on your thumb.

On a Winding Stick:
Firmly knot an end of the yarn onto the shaft of the winding stick so that you can easily hold on to the beginning of the skein.

Hold the winding stick in the left hand.

Wind a few times around the winding stick to get a "bun" to form the ball around.

Always wind in the same direction. Begin by laying the thread down at the lower right hand corner of the "bun" and then over the upper left corner. Turn the stick a little counterclockwise as you work so that each strand lies to the left of the previous one.

On the Thumb:
Wind around the thumb in the same way as on the winding stick. But, instead of turning the stick, slightly lift the ball off the thumb, turn it a little counterclockwise and then set it back down on the thumb again.

Winding Two Colors:
If you are using about the same amount of two colors for the knitting, you can wind them onto the same ball, one after the other. Wind one color first; knot its end with the end of the second color; continue winding the second color over the first. On a ball winder, it usually works well to wind two skeins into one ball, but that amount could be too heavy for a winding stick or your thumb.

Knit as usual with the outer and inner ends from the ball.

CASTING ON

Information Common to all three Methods of Casting On

Each set of instructions for two-end knitting has its own names for the various ways of casting on. I call them cast-on 1, 2, and 3.

The cast-on can seem very hard but don't be tempted to do it with bigger needles or over two needles as in regular knitting. All of these ways of casting on stretch out, as you will see.

If you cast on with a straight needle, the stitches should be slipped onto double points afterwards and not knitted from the straight needle. If you cast on to a circular needle, you can simply continue and knit the first row in the round after the cast-on row.

Securing the Yarn around the Ball

In two-end knitting, you twist the yarns around each other between every stitch, always working in the same direction. In order to be able to unwind the "back twist" which is built up, without drawing out more yarn, the ball must be bound in some way.

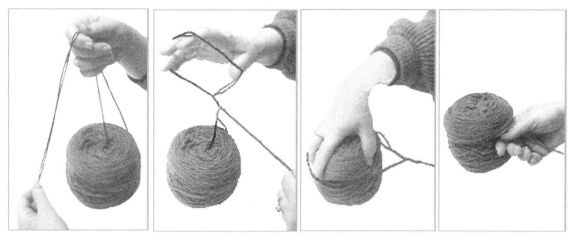

Draw out a couple of yards of each yarn end from the ball, turn them a couple of times around your hand so that a slip knot forms and lay it around the ball and draw it tight.

Common Beginning for all Three Methods of Casting On

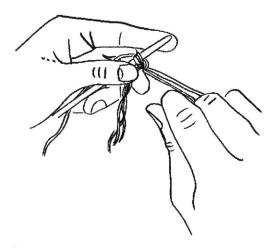

For all three methods of casting on, you will use 3 strands, both ends from the ball from which you will later knit, plus an extra strand. (In the first two cast-on methods, you can make a decorative edge by using a contrasting color for the extra strand.)

Make a slip knot with the three ends. Place the loop on a needle. The loop is only a way to start and will not be counted as a stitch. When the cast-on is finished, the loop is taken off the needle.

9

Cast-on Method 1

This is the easiest and most common method of casting on. It should always be used if the cast-on thread will be removed later, as, for example, with a skirt band.

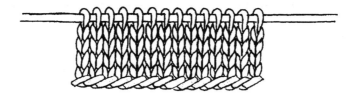

You have made a slip knot with the three yarn ends and placed the loop onto a needle.
Hold the needle in the left hand and steady it against your stomach.

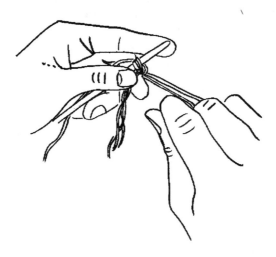

Hold the extra strand in your left hand and the strands with which you will knit in the right hand. For casting on and knitting, both strands are held in the right hand and separated by the middle finger.

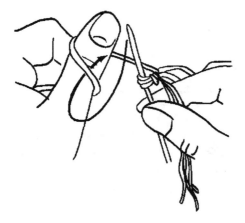

Place the left thumb in front of the extra strand and loop the strand around your thumb.

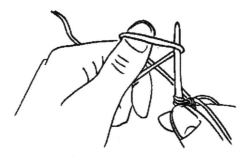

Insert the needle in the loop at the side of the thumb, with the point of the needle between the thumb and index finger of the left hand.

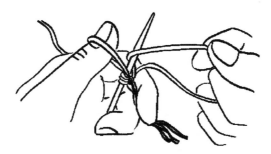

Pick up the backmost of the strands in the right hand with the index finger, bring it over the front strand and loop it around the point of the needle counterclockwise. At the same time, move the middle finger over the other strand so that both strands lie on the right side of the middle finger before the next stitch.

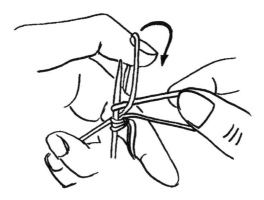

Grasp the needle with the thumb and index finger of the right hand, far enough down on the needle so that the strands in the right hand are pulled straight. Draw the loop on the left thumb over the point of the needle and pull on the extra strand.

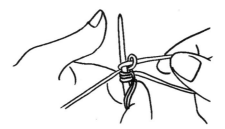

The stitch is complete. Begin the next stitch by looping the extra strand around the left thumb once again.

11

Cast-on Method 2

This cast-on method covers better than the first and holds the edge more firmly. It is the second most common cast-on but is, in my opinion, the best. It is formed in about the same way as the first cast-on except that you pick up the strands through the loop of the extra strand in a different way.

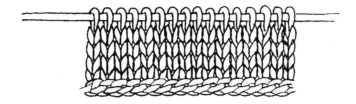

You have slip knotted the three strands into a loop and placed them on the needle.
Hold the needle in the left hand and steady it against your stomach.

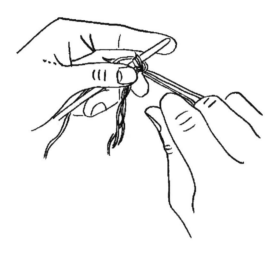

Hold the extra strand in the left hand and the strands for knitting in the right hand. These two strands are separated by the right hand's middle finger.

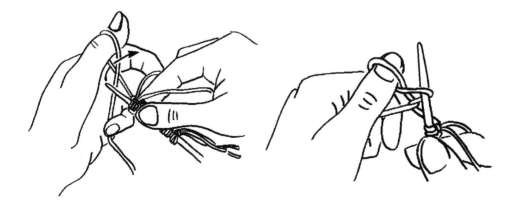

Loop the extra strand around the thumb and insert the needle behind the backmost strand in the loop around the thumb.

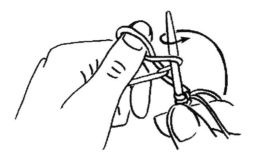

Pick up the backmost of the strands in the right hand with the index finger over the front strand and loop it around the point of the needle counterclockwise. At the same time, move the middle finger in the same way as for cast-on 1.

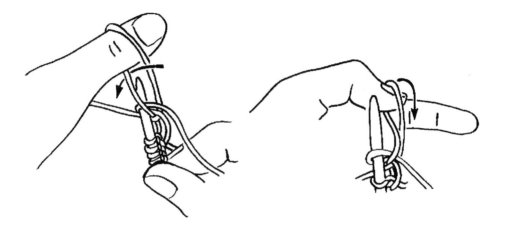

Insert the point of the needle back into the loop, draw the loop over and pull the extra strand taut.

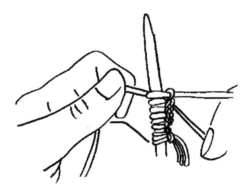

The stitch is complete. Repeat for the next stitch.

Cast-on Method 3

This cast-on method can be made with a single color or with three colors. There are descriptions of this in several places but I haven't tried them personally.

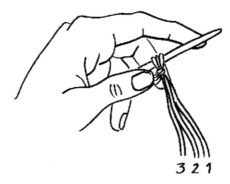

3 2 1

You have slip knotted the three strands into a loop which you have placed on a needle. This time, all three strands will be manipulated with the right hand. Hold the needle in the left hand and steady it against your stomach. (The drawing shows only how the needle is held and the order of the strands.)

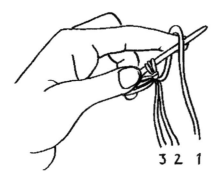

3 2 1

Hold the left index finger against the point of the needle. The front strand (1) is looped counterclockwise around the index finger and the needle.

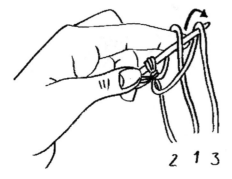

2 1 3

The backmost strand (3) is looped counterclockwise only over the point of the needle, so that it can build the stitch.

14

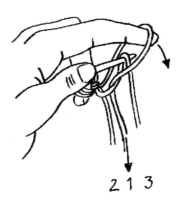

Loop the strand on the index finger over the point of the needle and pull it taut.

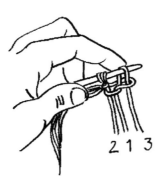

One stitch is complete.

Continue by laying the front strand over both the index finger and the point of the needle and the back strand only over the point of the needle. Loop it over and draw it taut.

KNITTING

For both casting on and knitting, the basic rule is that you always hold both strands in your right hand, separating them with the middle finger. When you are knitting, the needle is held in the left hand the whole time. The right needle is released every time you pick up a new strand.

Knit Stitches

When you are making knit stitches, the strands are held behind the work.

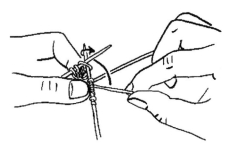

For a knit stitch, the needle is inserted as for a regular knit stitch. Release the needle, pick up the back strand with the index finger and bring it *over* the front strand. At the same time, lift the middle finger over the other strand so that the strands are in the correct position for the next stitch.

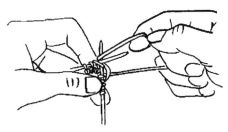

Loop the strand around the point of the needle counterclockwise.

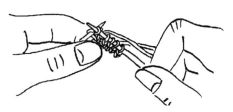

Grasp the right needle far enough down so that the strands are held taut and knit the stitch. Hold the needles at right angles to each other so that it will be easy to lift the completed stitch off the point of the needle without using the index finger to help.
On the charts, there is no symbol for the knit stitch – squares for knit stitches are blank.

Skewed Knit Stitches

One of my students wanted to knit a vest of straight pieces worked back and forth. By mistake, she twisted the strands around each other in the wrong direction. The result, however, was an interesting surface texture. The stitches leaned towards each other in different directions on the right side and the wrong side looked like a fishbone pattern.
The same thing can, of course, happen in regular knitting when you knit every other row in a different way. On the first row, work two-end knitting correctly but on the second row, bring the back strand under the front one. The strands should twist around each other in the "wrong direction" for the entire row.

17

Purl Stitches

When you work purl stitches, the strands are held in front of the work. The basic rules are the same as for knit stitches: both strands are held in the right hand and separated by the middle finger.

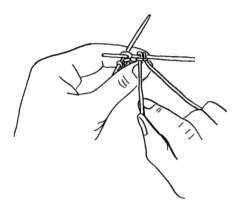

Insert the needle for a purl stitch exactly as in "regular" knitting.

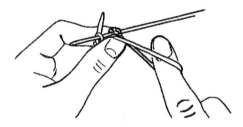

Release the needle and bring the back strand *under* the front one with the index finger. At the same time, lift the middle finger over the other strand so that the strands are in the correct position for the next stitch.

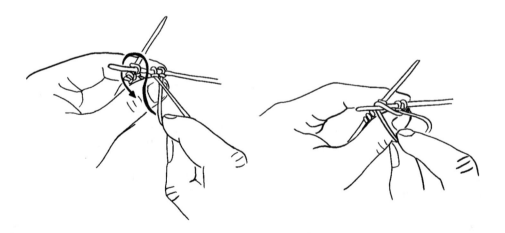

Loop the strand over the needle.

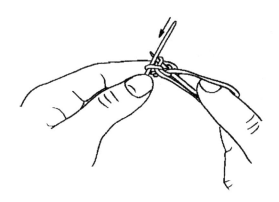

Grasp the needle far enough down so that the strands are held taut and complete the stitch. Hold the needles at right angles to each other so that it will be easy to lift the completed stitch off the point of the needle without using the index finger to help.

Single purl stitches are used for very discreet surface patterns.
A single purl row is used, for example, to frame a pattern group or to obtain a horizontal stripe effect.
On a chart, the purl stitches are indicated by a small circle.

Purl stitch █o█   Purl row █o█o█o█o█o█o█o█o█o█

Chart with purl and knit stitches

"Purl Braid"

Single Color

Work a regular two-end purl row. Work another purl row but bring the back strand over the front one. Twist the strands around each other in the "wrong direction" for the row.

Two-Color Braid

A "braid" in two colors is very decorative against a single-color background. Be sure that you have an even number of stitches. On the row before the braid is begun, work a knit row alternating the two colors 1 x 1. Then, work the braid as with a single color but alternating the colors in the sequence established on the knit row.

If the background is already a two-color stripe, then simply work the two braid rows.

Double Purl Stitches for a False Seam (also called Deep Purl Stitch)

Formerly, a false seam was knitted at the center back of stockings. Sewn stockings were considered finer than knitted ones so knitted stockings were worked to look as much as possible like sewn ones. One after the other, two purl stitches were worked, each with both strands held together. If both purl stitches were worked with twisted stitches the seam was deeper and more distinct.

On charts, the false seam is symbolized by a cross.

19

Hook (*Krok*) Stitches

Single-color curled patterns made with hook stitches are the most common and the prettiest way to decorate the surface.

You work hook stitches with one strand on each side of the right needle, without twisting between the stitches. However, you still hold the strands in your right hand and separate them with your middle finger.

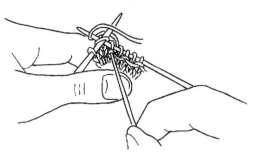

The knit stitches are worked on the wrong side

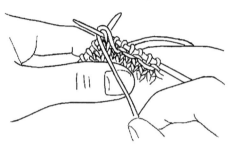

and the purl stitches on the right side.

A hook stitch consists of a group of stitches: purl-knit-purl.

Bring the back strand to the right side and purl it. Knit the next stitch with the strand held on the wrong side. Purl the last stitch with the strand on the right side and then put it on the wrong side. The strand between the purl stitches lies on top of the knit stitches and makes a "hook".

A circle in a pattern symbolizes a purl stitch. A dash does not mean, as one might suppose, a knit stitch. The dash means that the strand which is not used for the next stitch lies on top of the knit stitch.

Hook stitches are always worked knit over purl and purl over knit. If you work knit over knit and purl over purl, you will get totally normal double knitting with the wrong side facing out.

A whole row or several rows with hook stitches is called a hook row (*krok-varv*). It can be used as a single decorative row or in combination with several hook rows or hook patterns.

Two rows with hook stitches are called a chain path (*kedjegång*).

When you are working hook stitches or hook rows on double-pointed needles and have to change the needle in the middle of a pattern, work as follows:

Work to the end of the needle you are holding.

Put both strands on the wrong side of the piece.

Insert the new needle *between the strands* and then into the first stitch of the next needle; continue working.

When you are working several hook rows, one after the other, you must remember to cross the strands between rows when you have an even number of stitches.

If you are going to make a number of hook rows, one after the other, on a single-color garment, it is most efficient and will make an invisible row change if you work with an odd number of stitches. Decrease or increase one stitch before the hook row begins. If you are working with two colors and want a horizontal stripe effect, this won't work. The colors must be switched on every row.

Before you work a hook row or a chain in alternating colors, the new color should be knitted in on the row before. If you want a single-color chain row on a striped background, you should knit in both strands of the desired color on the row before.

	–	o	–		
	o	–	o		

This little pattern motif is called an "O". It is worked over 2 rows. The first row is worked purl-knit-purl. On the second row, bring the front strand for the purl stitch to the right side and work knit-purl-knit and put the strand from the purl stitch to the wrong side.

					o						
				o	–	o					
			o	–	o	–	o				
		o	–	o		o	–	o			
	o	–	o				o	–	o		
		o	–	o		o	–	o			
			o	–	o	–	o				
				o	–	o					

A hook pattern looks the best when you finish with a single purl stitch row after the last row with purl-knit-purl. This makes a point to finish off the hook under the knit stitches. At the beginning of a hook stitch pattern, the strand between the purl stitches bends downwards so a purl row before it is not necessary as it wouldn't be seen.

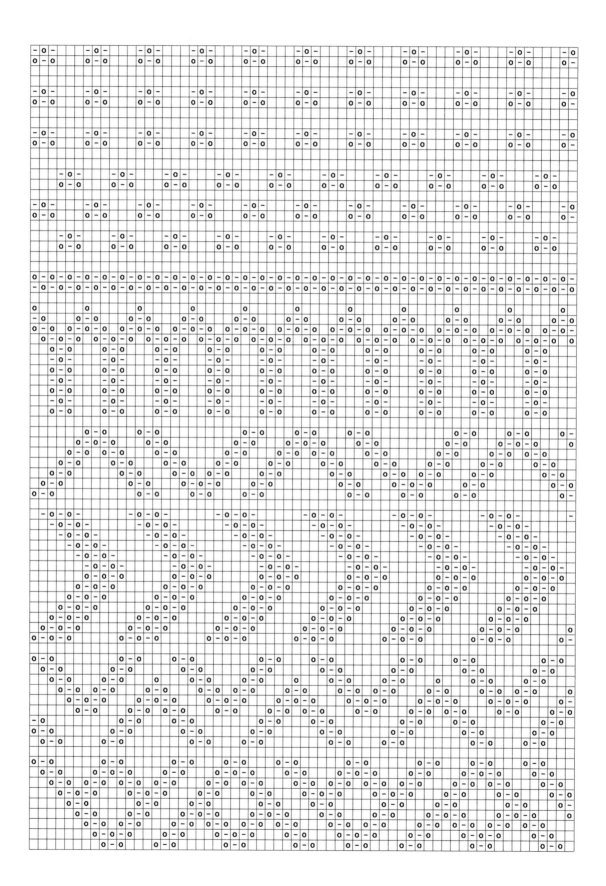

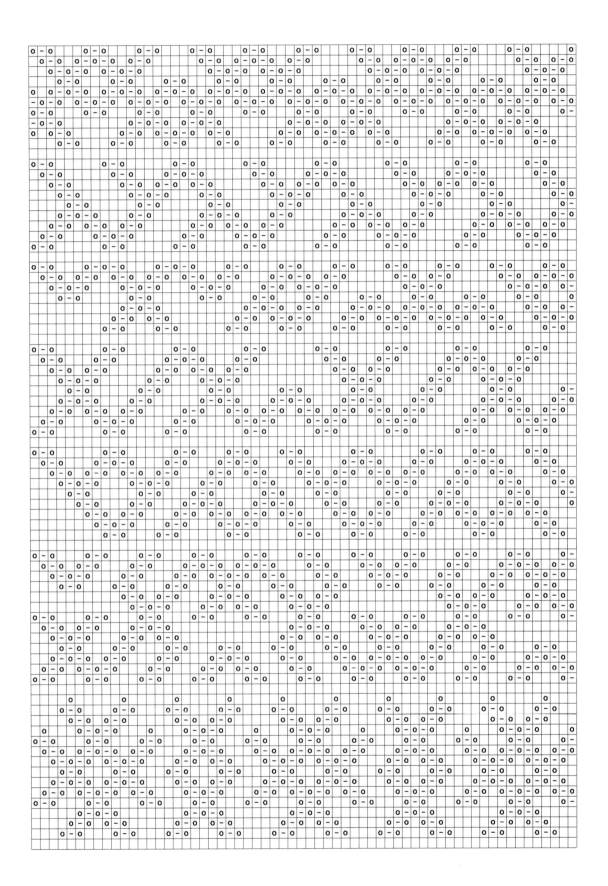

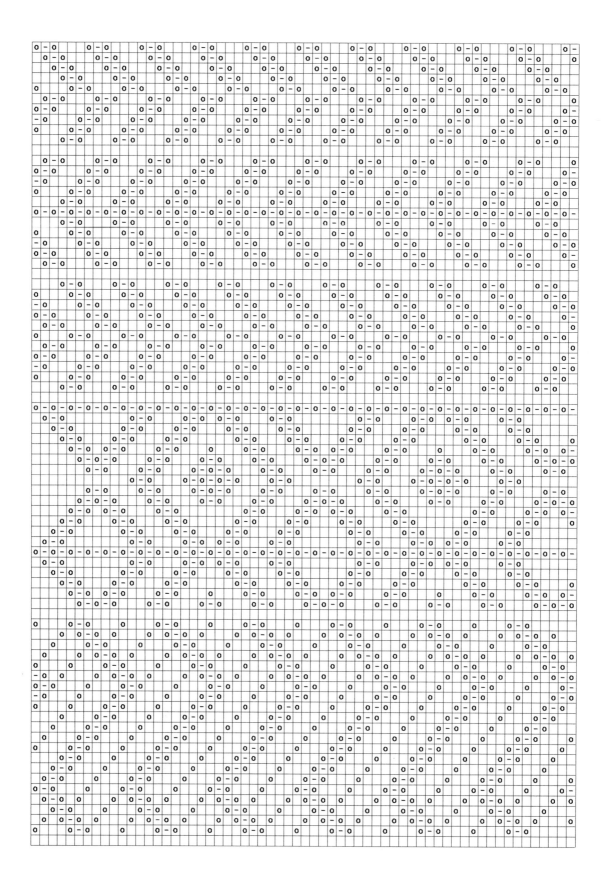

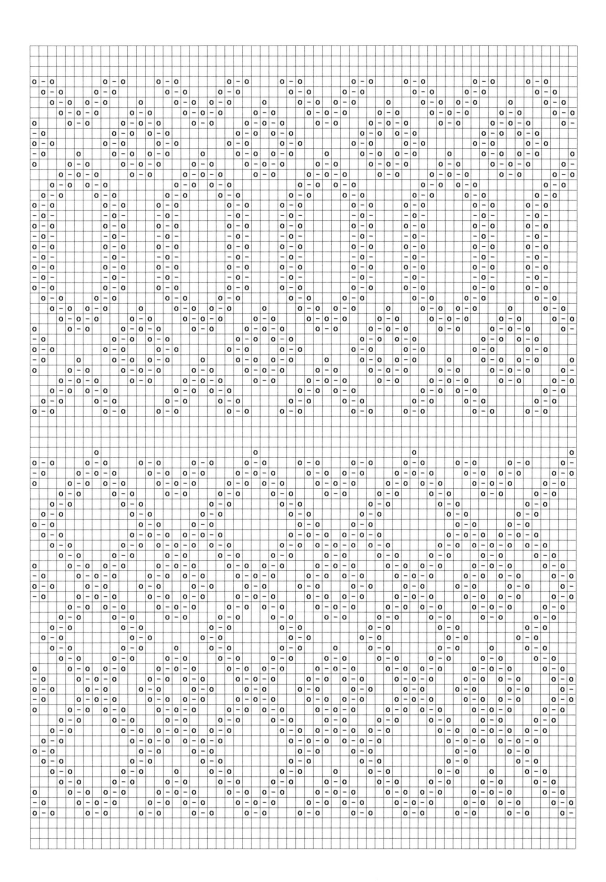

Deep Stitches

Deep stitches are used in the same way as purl stitches for making discreet surface patterns. They are called deep stitches when you bring the strand not being knitted with to the front, to lie in front of and cover a knit stitch. I have never heard an explanation for the name of the stitch.

If you want to work *every alternate* stitch as a deep stitch, work as follows:
Before the deep stitch is worked, bring the front strand between the needles and hold it on the right side of the work.
Knit a stitch with the other strand on the wrong side.
Put the strand lying on the right side back on the wrong side.

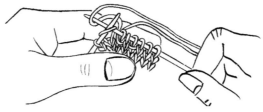

and knit the next stitch with *that* strand and without twisting the strands.
For the next deep stitch, bring that *same* strand to the right side once again.
Knit a stitch with the strand on the wrong side.
Bring the strand from the right side back to the wrong side and knit the next stitch with it. Continue as described above.

On the charts, a deep stitch is indicated by a dash.
The dash means that the strand with which you are not knitting the next stitch (the front strand) is brought to the right side before the knit stitch is worked.

If you are working a pattern with several deep stitches, one after the other, you should cross the strands between each stitch. It doesn't matter whether the strands are crossed over or under each other; it is important that you always cross them in the same way so that the slant of the deep stitches will always be in the same direction.
Deep stitches are most often used for marking an edge or for framing a pattern of hook stitches. In that case, it is worked over only 2-3 stitches.

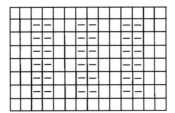

A simulated ribbing can be made with 2 deep stitches + 2 knit stitches worked around the row. It is not, however, a true ribbing.

COLOR PATTERNS

With Two Colors

Striped – Checked

If you knit with one strand of each color and an even number of stitches, the pattern will be striped. With an odd number of stitches, the pattern is checked.

If you knit two stitches with the same color next to each other, the colors move a step and shift in relation to each other. Simple and pretty patterns can be made from such shifts.

Patterns with a strand of each color.

If both colors are closely and regularly used throughout a pattern, I knit with one strand of each color. If you follow the rules exactly, then the strands should be twisted between every stitch. The risk with this method is that a dark or strong color will show through, so it is best to twist after two stitches.

If you want three stitches of one color and one stitch of the other, knit two stitches after each other with the first color without twisting. Then twist it with the second color and knit the third stitch with the first color. Finally, the stitch with the second color is knitted. As I see it, it is allowable to cheat a little. However, don't work more than two stitches after each other before twisting. Otherwise, it will be like regular single-strand knitting.

Patterns with two strands of the background color and one strand of the pattern color.

If one color is used more often than the other in a pattern, I knit with two strands of the background color and one strand of the pattern color. There are various ways of holding the strands. I think that it is easiest to two-end knit with both strands of the background color and do regular knitting with one strand of the pattern color. The pattern color is held over the left index finger. There should not be long carries lying loosely on the wrong side, so the pattern color should be rather taut. See "Catching in a Pattern Strand" (p. 42) for learning how to secure long carries.

With two strands of the background color and a little pattern motif in another color.

If you want to have a little pattern motif at the side of a thumb gusset on a mitten or only a little colored motif in an otherwise single-color background, you lay in a strand which will not be carried for the whole row.
For a round or V-shaped motif, knit the strand in at the center so each end can be worked up.
For a straight-up motif over one or a couple of stitches, use only one end of the strand and carry it up.

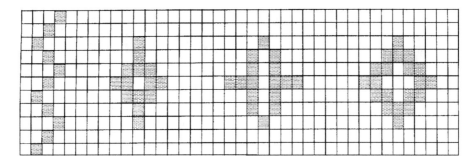

Hook or Deep Stitches with Two Colors

I have worked a considerable amount with two-colored curled patterns, a combination of color and surface pattern, which one of my students christened "Labyrinth Pattern." The technique is worked so that two colors are used to make a striped background upon which a pattern of hook or deep stitches covers the stitch's color in the background. I originally got the idea for this type of patterning from the designs called Mosaic knitting in regular knitting.

Because both colors are used for all of the knitting, I wind each of them into the same ball. Knit as usual with the outer and inner strands from the ball with an even number of stitches.

Precisely as for single-color curled patterns, the hook stitches must be worked with a knit stitch over a purl and a purl over a knit. It follows that the horizontal lines also are formed with alternating colors if you work the pattern on every row. If you knit with deep or hook stitches only every other row, you can produce single-color squares or wider single-color stripes on a striped background.

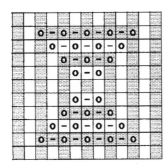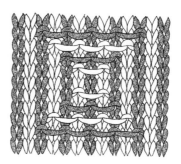

I have indicated the hook stitches with the normal o-o; the knit stitches in between are not symbolized.

If the squares are shaded dark, then the purl stitches of the hook stitches are worked with the dark color.

If the squares are white, then the purl stitches of the hook stitches are worked with the light color.

At the right is a drawing which shows a section of a knitted pattern.

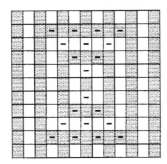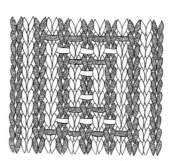

If deep stitches are substituted for the hook stitches, the result will be similar but with a different surface structure, almost like weaving.
I have indicated the deep stitches with – and the knit stitches in between are not symbolized.

The pattern is made by working every other stitch as a regular knit stitch and the alternate stitches as a deep stitch. The color of the deep stitch's strand "covers over" the color of the knit stitch.

On the following 4 pattern charts, the left side shows how the pattern should be worked. On the right side, I've illustrated how the final result will look. On the remaining pattern charts, you can decide for yourself whether you want to work them with hook or deep stitches.

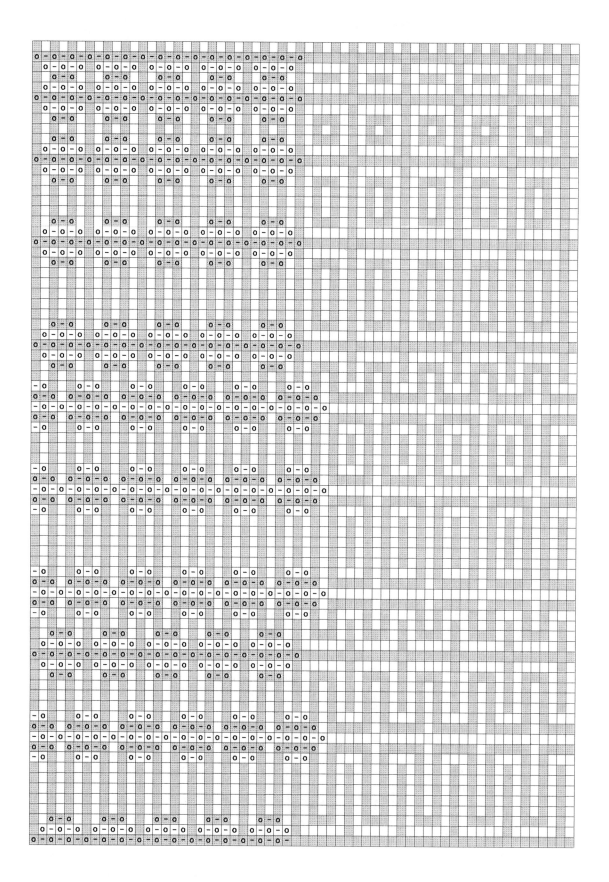

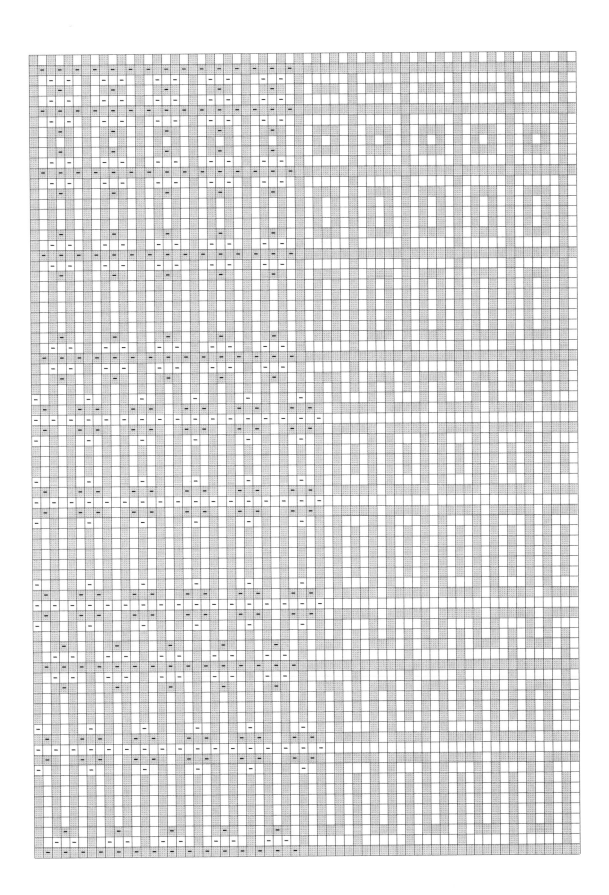

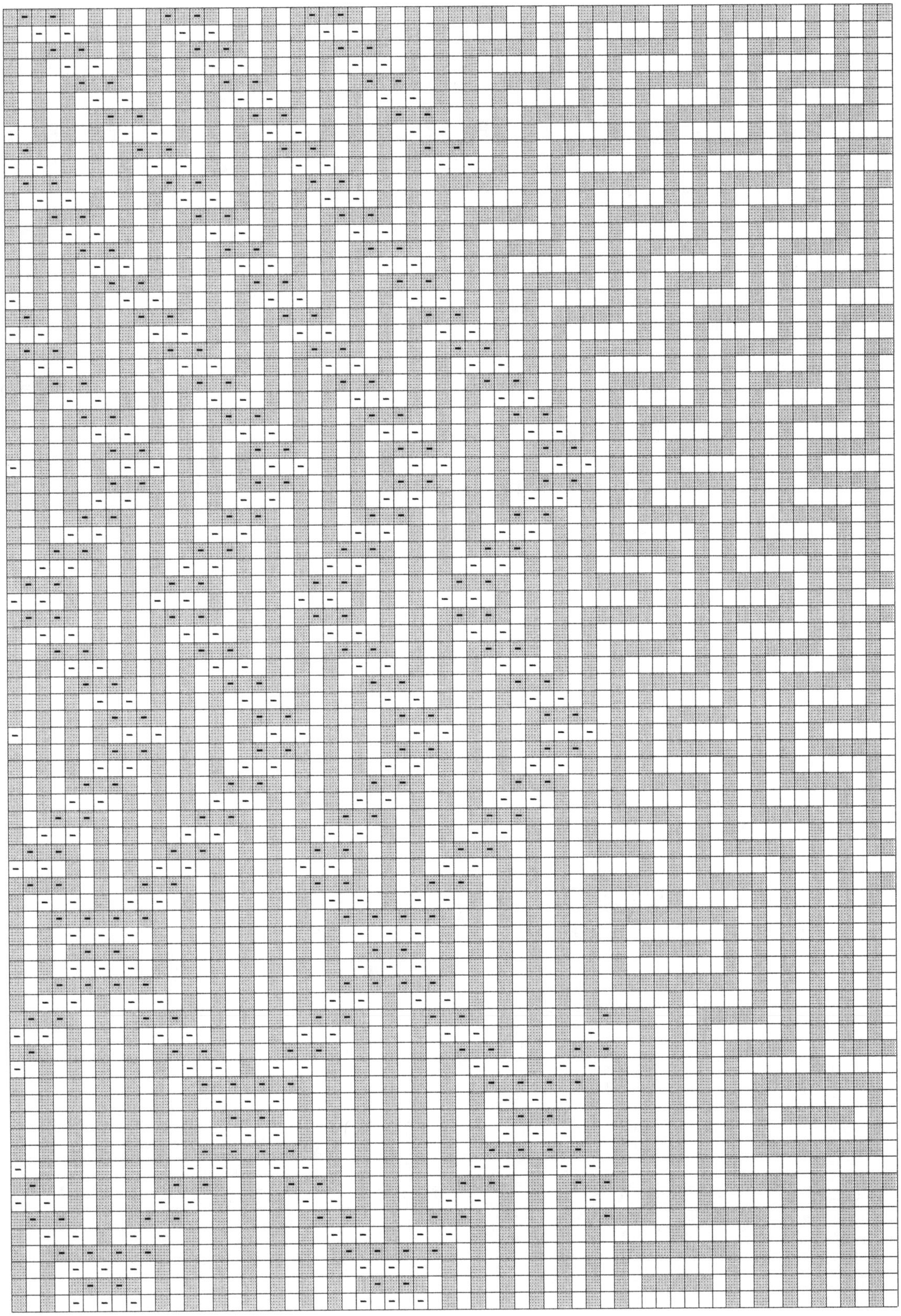

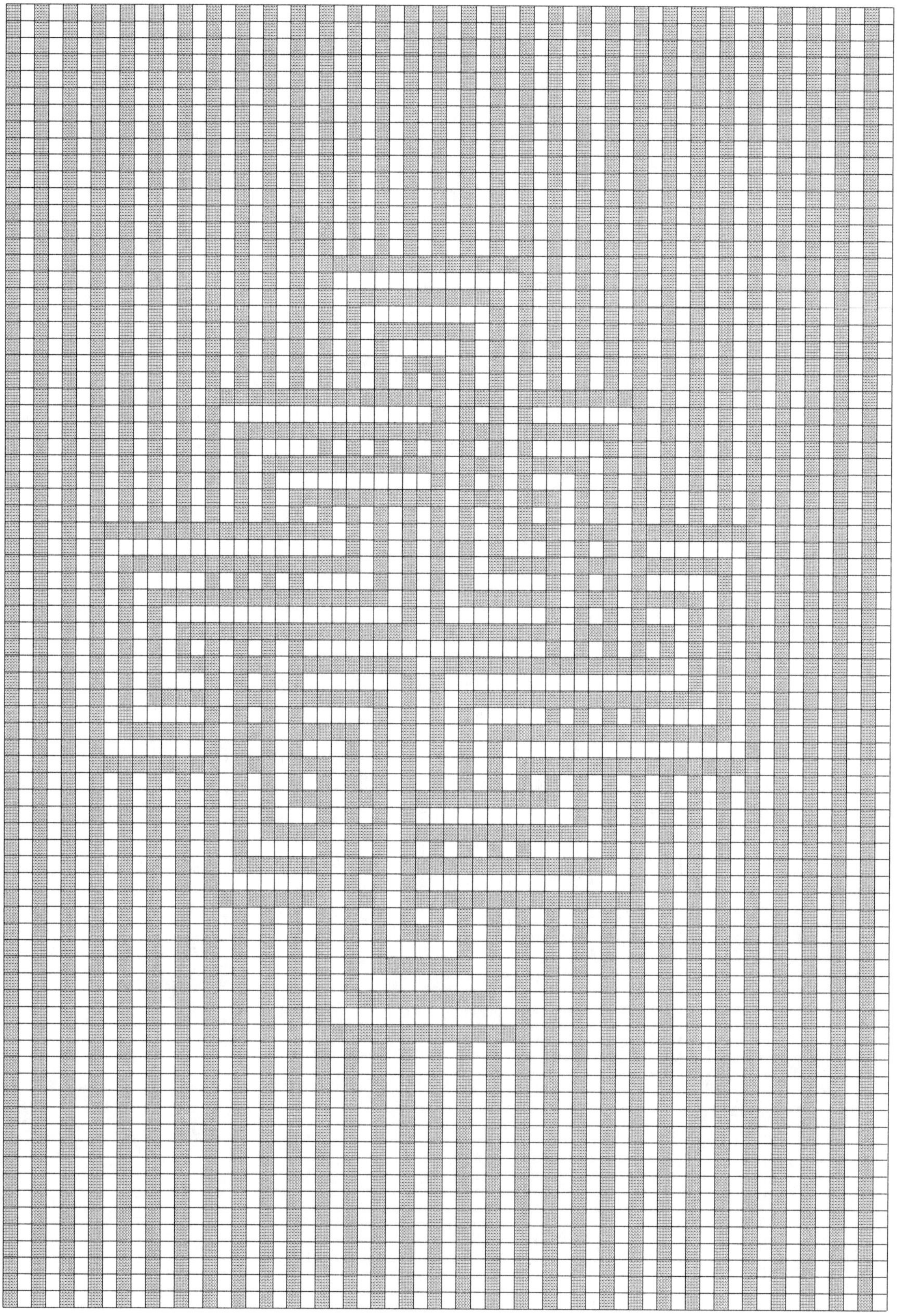

With Three Colors

If you want to knit with three colors and all three colors are used in approximately equal amounts, the backmost strand must be twisted forward on each stitch. Make three small bobbins of yarn which can hang free of each other. Because the strands are twisted as needed, all three strands must be held in the air at the same time so that they can twist around each other again.

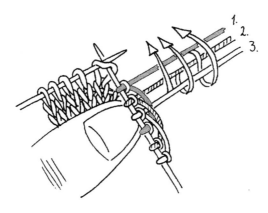

Starting position

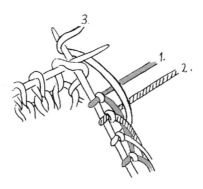

If color number 3 is needed for a stitch, bring it forward over numbers 1 and 2 and knit it. Be sure and keep the strands separated!

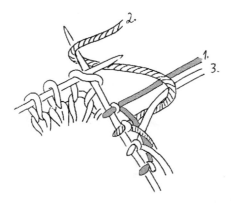

If color number 2 is needed for a stitch, bring it back under number 3 and then over number 1.

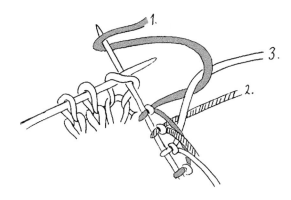

If color number 1 is needed for a stitch, bring the strand back over number 2 and under number 3 which will then come forward when number 1 is knitted.

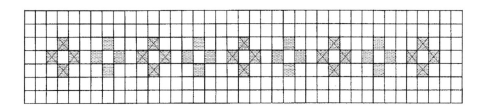

Catching in a Pattern Strand

Do not let a pattern strand lie loosely on the wrong side over more than 2 stitches without catching it in as the third stitch is knitted.

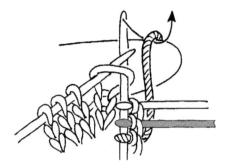

Insert the right needle into the third stitch but do not knit it.

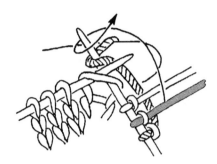

Bring the pattern strand over the point of the right needle next to the stitch just begun.

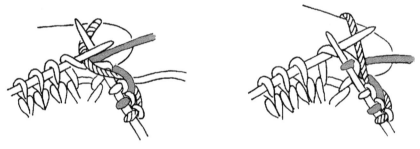

The pattern strand lies on the needle next to the stitch as if it were also a stitch but it is not knitted through. Only work the actual stitch.

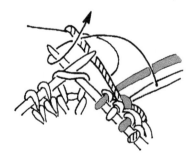

Hold the pattern strand over the left index finger when the stitch is knitted. When it has been knitted, the pattern strand will be caught in the twist on the wrong side.

In regular single-strand knitting, strands are caught by picking them up and catching them with the left needle on the next row.

KNITTING TECHNIQUES

Increasing Single Stitches

To increase a single stitch, knit a stitch with both strands at the same time. You can bring both strands to the needle at the same time, but should place the strands on the needle in the same order as when you are knitting. Bring one strand at a time to the needle. The advantage when working with two colors is that the strands can easily be arranged in the right order on the needle. On the next row, the strands are knitted separately and one stitch is increased to two.

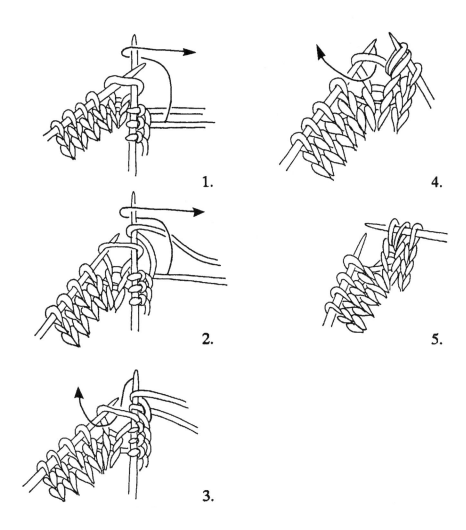

1.

2.

3.

4.

5.

If you are knitting with two colors, be sure to twist the strands so that the colors come out in the correct order.

Casting On Several Stitches within the Work

In making a garment, you will sometimes need to cast on several stitches one after the other within a piece. This can be done in several ways. I think that this is the easiest:

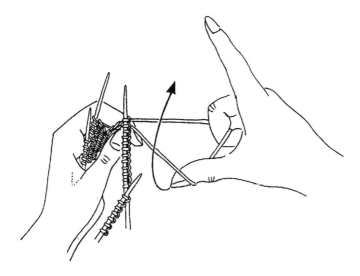

Hold the right needle in the left hand with the point straight out in front of you.
Hold the strands as usual in the right hand with the middle finger in between them.
Place the thumb upwards, in front of the back strand (and also between the strands).

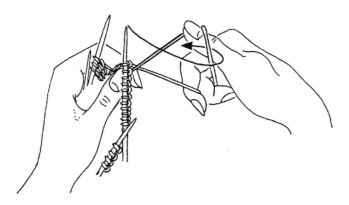

Turn the thumb down-back-up so that the back strand is twisted in a half loop around the thumb.

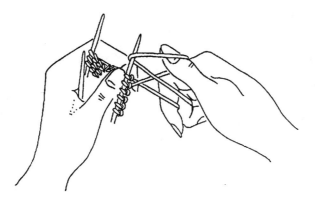

Place the loop just made onto the needle.

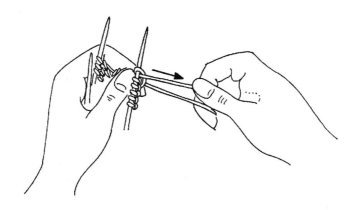

Pull taut.

Now the second strand is the one most far back. Bring the index finger over and work in the same manner. Continue until you have cast on the desired number of stitches.

The first row after the cast-on might be difficult to knit but it shouldn't be too difficult.

Picking Up and Knitting Stitches from the Loops

When you have removed the knitted- or sewn-in thread for the thumbholes on mittens or the foot of a stocking, you have live stitches on one side and loops on the other. You can simply place the live stitches on a needle. New stitches must be picked up from the loops. The same thing applies after a cast-on within the piece. If you use the loops as if they were stitches, you will get holes.

I pick up the stitches with only one strand because I think it is too unseemly to use both. A single-color horizontal stripe in striped knitting cannot be avoided. The second strand can be brought in after the picking up and knitting, and then you can continue knitting around.

Begin and end far enough out on the edge so that you have two extra stitches. On the next row, you can knit the first and last picked up stitches together with a stitch on either side of them. In this way, small holes, which must otherwise be sewn together, are avoided.

Work as follows:

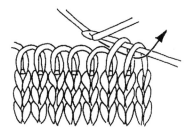

Pick up two loops with a crochet hook. Draw the strand through and place the new stitch on a needle.

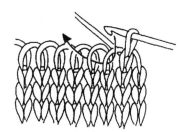

To continue, pick up the second loop from the previous "stitch" at the same time as you pick up the next new loop.

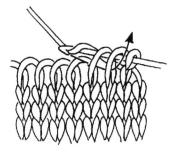

Draw the strand through for a new stitch each time and place it on the needle.
If the stitches end up facing the wrong direction on the needle, they should be turned to face correctly before they are knitted on the first row around.

Or in this way:

Pick up all the loops onto a needle.
Knit together the first two stitches with one strand.
For the next stitch, place loop number 2 back on the needle and knit it together with loop number 3. Continue with loops 3+4, 4+5, 5+6, etc.

Decreasing

When you knit mittens, stockings and caps, you have to work decreases in order to shape the piece correctly. Decreases are made in the same way as for regular knitting. The method you use for decreasing will determine how visible and noticeable or how discreet the decreases will be. Where you place the decreases is sometimes determined by the piece (for example, on mittens and stocking feet) but sometimes you can decide how to place the decreases in order to create a pattern (as, for example, on caps).

When you decrease, choose one of the alternatives listed below and take into consideration the direction the decrease should lean in.

Decreasing 1 stitch:

1. Insert the right needle into the front loops of 2 stitches and knit them together to make 1 stitch. The decrease leans to the right.

2. Insert the right needle into the back loops of 2 stitches and knit them together to make 1 stitch. The decrease leans to the left.

3. Slip a stitch knitwise. Knit the next stitch. Pass the slipped stitch over the knitted one. The decrease leans to the left.

   A common decrease which is placed at the beginning of the first and third needles and at the end of the second and fourth needles is called a *band decrease.*
   First and third needles: Knit one stitch and knit the next two stitches together through the back loops.
   Second and fourth needles: Knit until three stitches remain; knit the next two stitches together through the front loops; knit the last stitch.

Decreasing 2 stitches at the same time:

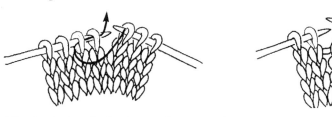

4. Slip 2 stitches knitwise at the same time.

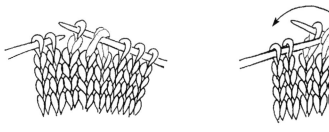

Knit the next stitch and pass both slipped stitches over it at the same time.

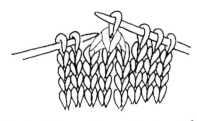

The decrease is straight up. The outer two of the three stitches lie behind the center stitch.

47

The most practical way to make an invisible decrease on a hook row is as follows: slip a purl and a knit stitch knitwise at the same time; knit the next purl stitch and pass the slipped stitches over. The decrease is not visible behind the loops between the two purl stitches.

5. A little more complicated way to decrease which gives the same result as the previous one only works at the gap between two needles: at the beginning of a needle, take a new needle and slip the first two stitches to it through the back loops – from right to left – turn the needle so that you can pick up the stitch knitted last on the previous needle – turn the needle back – bring the knitted stitch through the two slipped ones.

6. You can make a straight decrease where the stitches will lean towards each other invisibly if you slip two stitches through front loops and draw the stitch knitted just beforehand through both slipped loops.

7. Slip a stitch knitwise. Insert the right needle into the front loops of the next two stitches and knit them together into one stitch. Pass the slipped stitch over the decreased stitch. This decrease will appear to lean to the left but is straight.

8. Insert the right needle in the front loops of the next two stitches and knit them together into one stitch. Slip a stitch knitwise. Pass the decreased stitch over the slipped stitch. This decrease will appear to lean to the right but is straight.

<u>Binding Off</u>

Binding off is done as for regular single-strand knitting. Use only a single strand and bind off more tightly than usual. With some yarns, you have to pull the stitches more tightly so that they will not be too loose.

<u>Finishing</u>

There are many different ways of finishing a mitten or the toes and heels of socks, just as there are for regular knitting.

1. Cut yarn and thread end through a blunt tapestry needle. Thread through the stitches in order and pull them into a circle. Weave in end on wrong side.

2. Divide the stitches evenly onto two needles and hold the needles parallel. Cut yarn and thread through a blunt tapestry needle. Weave stitches together by alternately threading through a stitch from one needle and then the other.

3. Finishing method 2 will look better if you first turn the work to the wrong side.

4. Divide the stitches evenly onto two needles and cut one of the strands. Knit the first stitch on each needle together. Knit the next stitch on each needle together. Now you have two stitches on the right needle. Pass the back one over the front one as for regular binding off. Knit two together using a stitch from each needle and bind them off. Cut thread and pull end through the last stitch.

5. Turn the whole piece so that the wrong side faces out. Arrange the stitches on two needles. Pass the stitches on the back needle over those on the front needle one by one. Half of the original number of stitches now remains. Bind them off as usual, using only one strand. Cut yarn and pull end through the last stitch.

6. Turn the whole piece so that the wrong side faces out. Arrange the stitches on two needles. Knit two together taking a stitch from each needle. Half of the original number of stitches now remains. Bind them off as usual, using only one strand. Cut yarn and pull end through the last stitch.

7. Divide the stitches evenly onto two needles. Hold the work in the left hand and begin to pick up from the back with a third needle. Pick up one stitch from the back needle and one from the front. Pass the first stitch over the second. Pick up a new stitch from each needle. Now there are 3 stitches on the right needle. Pass the middle stitch over the front one. Then pass the back stitch over the front one. Now there is one stitch remaining on the right needle again. Continue by picking up two new stitches—pass over the middle one – pass over the back one. Continue in this manner until one stitch remains. Cut yarn and pull end through the last stitch.

Turned or Short Rows

Technically, it works fine to two-end knit a straight piece back and forth as in regular knitting but it can feel troublesome. It is obviously more comfortable to knit in the round for as long as possible.

In order to shape a garment, you might have to knit one piece a bit longer than the other. In that case, I don't knit around the entire row but turn it several times to the side of the piece which doesn't need more rows. To avoid ugly holes which can result from the turning, certain techniques are needed.

Each time you turn, you must make a yarn-over and slip a stitch.
This is done in slightly different ways for the right and wrong sides.
Every time you come to an earlier turn, the yarn-over and the next stitch must be knitted together. This is also done in different ways for the right and wrong sides.

Turning from the Right to the Wrong Side

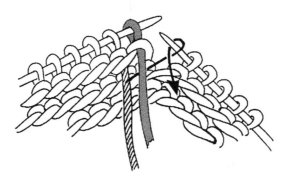

Turn the entire piece from the right side and hold it so that you can work on the wrong side.

Make the yarn-over with the strand which at the far left. First, bring the strand under the front strand and then over and around the right needle counterclockwise. Slip the next stitch from the back through the back loop.

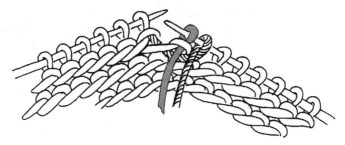

Purl and begin with the strand used in the yarn-over.

50

Turning from the Wrong to the Right-Side

Turn the entire piece from the wrong side and hold it so that you can work on the right side.

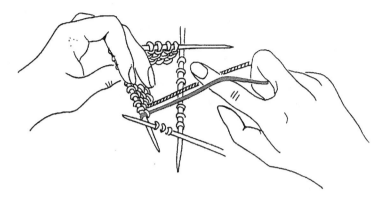

Make the yarn-over with the strand which lies to the far left.

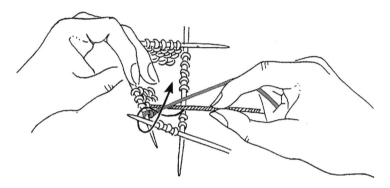

This time, the strand for the yarn-over is brought under the front strand, from between the needles

and back over the right needle.
Slip a stitch knitwise.

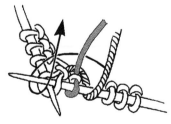

The next stitch is knitted with the strand used in the yarn-over but the strand must first be brought under the strand from the slipped stitch (you have to twist the strands around each other in the wrong direction this once).

Continue knitting across.

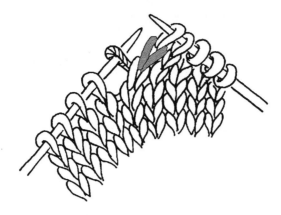

Knit up to the yarn-over on the previous row. The slipped stitch on the previous row will have been knitted.

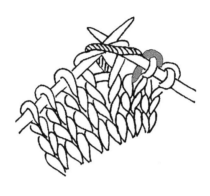

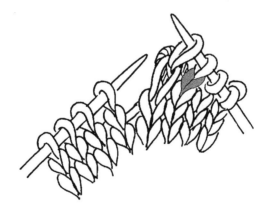

Knit the yarn-over with the next stitch, making one knit stitch.

Working the Stitches Together at the Turn on the Wrong Side

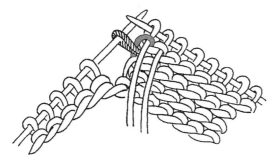

Purl up to the yarn-over on the previous row. The slipped stitch on the previous row will have been purled.

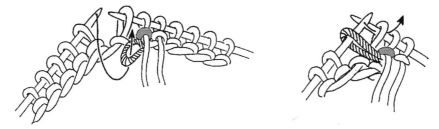

Shift the placement of the yarn-over from the previous row with that of the next stitch. Cross the stitches so that the yarn-over lies on the wrong side.

Purl the stitches together, making one purl stitch.

On the first knit row around, after all the turns have been completed, the last turn on the wrong side will be knitted together. In this place, the yarn-over must be crossed with the next stitch so that the yarn-over lies on the wrong side. The stitches are knitted together to make a knit stitch.

In certain situations, for example, when shaping the back of a pair of pants, all of the turns are made first and then, finally, there is one row for working them together. In that way, all of the holes are closed on just one row.

Cutting Knitted Pieces Open

It is less risky cutting two-end knitting than regular knitting because the stitches do not separate as easily. However, as for regular knitting, the stitches must be bound with a seam on each side of the line to be cut. I think the seam is more flexible if sewn by hand rather than by machine. Don't press the seam on the knitted material too hard or the edge will become wavy.

When figuring the total number of stitches for a piece, add in 7 stitches for the edge or steek. There will be one stitch at the center to cut; two stitches on each side of the center to sew; and then an additional stitch at each side in which to pick up stitches for the edging or to turn under. If the edge is to be turned under, it is advisable to purl that stitch all the way up the piece. Remember not to knit the pattern over these 7 stitches.

On a piece that I am going to cut, I usually bind off with a supplementary yarn to avoid cutting the binding off. Work up to the stitch before the one in which you will cut and take out the yarn. Put the stitch to be cut onto a coilless safety pin or a bit of yarn. Begin binding off on the next stitch with a new strand.

The cut edge must be covered and there are several ways of doing this. A knitted edging should be worked in regular single-strand knitting because two-end knitting is too bulky when turned under.

For most yarns, the proportions will be correct if you pick up and knit 1 stitch each in 2 rows and then skip a row and pick up and knit in the next two rows (= 2 stitches for every 3 rows). Pick up and knit the stitches on the right side. Knit as many rows as desired for the width of the edging. Make a purl row for the turning, and then knit the same number of rows as before the turning. Don't forget the buttonholes. Sew the edge securely to the wrong side. Use the same size needle as the one the garment was knitted with.

It is easier to ensure that the edge will be nice and flat if you wash the garment before you cut it open.

Sweater with the Back and Front the Same

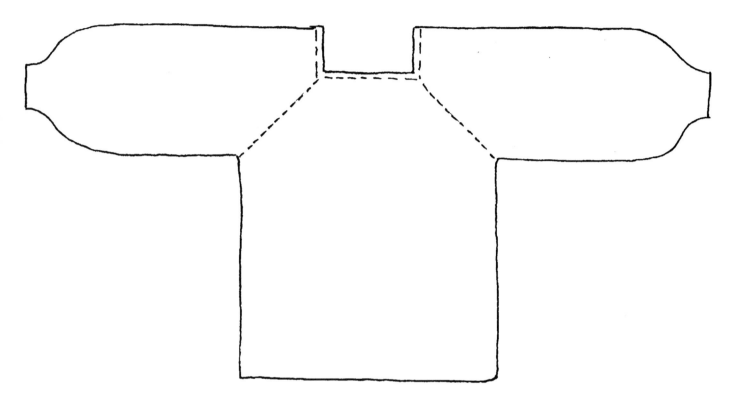

Sweater with a Shaped Neck

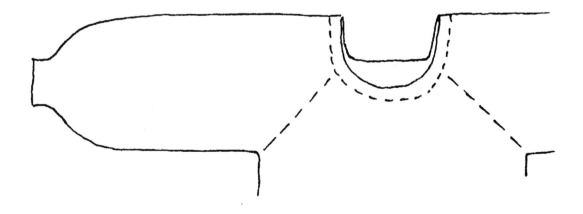

Calculating

It is quite fun to design your own garments and it isn't hard if you have a good idea and are careful. It is most important to be very careful in counting the number of stitches per row and rows per centimeter/inch with the yarn you will be using. It is not sufficient to count the stitches and rows over just one centimeter or inch.

A swatch which you will measure and count must be at least 7 x 7 cm/3 x 3 inches. Hold the measuring tape in from the edge of the swatch and count how many stitches and rows there are in 5 cm/2 inches. Divide the total by 5/2 so that you know how many stitches there are in 1 cm/1 inch. If the stitch count in 5 cm is 16 stitches, then the stitch gauge is 16 : 5 = 3.2 stitches/cm. If I am going to cast on a circular piece that is 60 cm around, I figure 60 x 3.2 = 192 stitches. If I had been careless about the gauge and rounded it down to 3 stitches/cm, then I would have figured 60 x 3 = 180 stitches to be cast on. The difference is 192-180 = 12 stitches off. That would mean 60 – (180 : 3.2) = 3.75 cm short in the circumference. That is a whole size too small on a garment.

Do not skip making a gauge swatch!

Here are some formulas for figuring out the information you will need for determining the numbers for a pattern.

Number of stitches: number of cm/inches = stitch gauge

Number of cm/inches x stitch gauge = number of stitches

Number of stitches: stitch gauge = the number of cm/inches

Number of rows: number of cm/inches = row gauge

Number of cm/inches x row gauge = number of rows

Number of rows: row gauge = number of cm/inches

Next, you need to consider the measurements for the garment you want to knit. It is easiest to measure a garment you already have and feel comfortable in. The size of the yarn should be about the same for both garments. If you don't have a garment to measure, you can measure your own body. Don't forget to add in a few centimeters/inches for ease. How much you should add depends on the thickness of the yarn and the style of fit desired. Thinner garments need less ease than heavier ones.

An Example of How to Calculate the Numbers

Converting Instructions

You might, perhaps, have a pattern which recommends a certain size of yarn but you want to knit the garment with a different size yarn.

For example, you have instructions using a yarn with a gauge of 3.2 stitches and 2.8 rows per cm but you want to knit with a much finer yarn which has a gauge of 4.6 stitches and 4.2 rows per cm. You have cast on 176 stitches with the heavier yarn. In order to figure out how many stitches you need with the thinner yarn, you take:

The number of stitches: the heavy yarn's stitch gauge x the thin yarn's stitch gauge = the new number of stitches. For example, 176 : 3.2 x 4.6 = 253 stitches needed with the thin yarn.

You have knitted 56 rows with the heavy yarn. How many rows do you need with the thin yarn to get the same length?

The number of rows: the heavy yarn's row gauge x the thin yarn's row gauge = the new row gauge. That is, for example: 56 : 2.8 x 4.2 = 84 rows with the thin yarn.

Calculating the Decreases on a Drop Sleeve.

On a drop sleeve, the decreases are divided more or less evenly down the length of the sleeve. You should always knit a few rows at the beginning and end of a sleeve without any decreases.

Subtract the number of stitches you want to remain when the sleeve is finished from the number on the needles at the beginning so that you will know how many stitches to decrease. Because it works best to decrease 1 stitch on each side of the sleeve "seam," divide the number of stitches to be decreased in half. Then you know how many times you have to decrease.

Now figure out how many rows long the sleeve will be. The number of cm/inches from the armhole to the wrist is multiplied with the row gauge which will give you the total number of rows to be worked. Take away the number of rows at the beginning and end which will not have any decreases. Figure out how closely you want the decreases to be spaced to decrease the number of stitches you desire. Divide the row count you have remaining with the number of decreases which need to be made.

An example for a drop sleeve:

Stitch count before decreasing: 160
Desired stitch count after decreasing: 90
Number of stitches which need to be decreased: 160 – 90 = 70
Number of decreases: 70 : 2 = 35 stitches
Total sleeve length: 50 cm
Row gauge: 2.9 rows per cm
Total number of rows: 50 x 2.9 = 145
Decreases divided down the total length: 145 rows : 35 times = decease every 4th row with 5 rows left over. 5 rows without decreasing are too few so you should decrease every 3rd row.
Decreasing every 3rd row 35 times: 3 x 35 = 105 rows
Rows remaining to divide before and after the decrease rows: 145 – 105 = 40 rows
It should be okay to knit 35 rows before beginning to decrease and have 5 rows remaining after the decreases.
That makes 35 : 2.9 = about 11 cm before and 5 : 2.9 = about 2 cm after the last decrease row

PLANNING

Knitting Large Garments

It is not more difficult to knit a large garment, such as a sweater, jacket, or skirt in two-end knitting, than to knit mittens or socks; there are just many more stitches. Keep in mind, however, how much time-consuming work it is knitting a large garment. Plan carefully before beginning so that you can avoid an unfortunate result.

If you have a yarn in hand which you haven't knitted with before, it would not be wise to begin immediately on a large garment. First, knit a good-sized gauge swatch in stockinette or try out the yarn on a cap with only a little curled stitch patterning. If the gauge swatch is patterned with many curled stitches, you will not get the same gauge as with stockinette.

Two-end knitting does not have the same tendency to roll up on the edges as regular knitting does. Nevertheless, it is nice to finish a lower edge on a sweater or skirt with some curled stitch patterning. Even one repeat of chain stitch or a purl row can be sufficient. When a garment has just been finished, it may look like the edge will roll up or look unruly but that will correct itself after washing.

On sweaters with raglan sleeves, I knit them in one combined piece beginning at the cast-on for the neck. To begin with, I knitted that way because I hadn't learned that there is another way to do this in regular knitting. In two-end knitting, it is a great advantage to knit in this fashion because you will want to work in the round for as long as possible. Another advantage is that, whenever you want to, you can put the stitches onto a waste yarn and try the garment on to be sure that it fits well. You also can avoid sewing pieces together afterwards.

When you are knitting sweaters and other large garments, it is important to consider the correct placement of patterning. Think about which part of a pattern will look best, for example, at the center front. When I begin a sweater, I make sure that the pattern looks balanced at the center front and back and on each of the sleeves. At the increase lines for raglan sleeves, it comes out as it comes out. Personally, I never work patterning over the raglan lines because it only looks muddled.

If you want a pattern to begin at the neckline and finish just under the bustline, you need to knit the pattern a little further down on the sleeves. Otherwise, there is a risk that the sweater will look outgrown. If you finish the pattern before dividing the sections, there won't be any problem.

I knitted my first sweater without considering that the front and back pieces actually needed to be different lengths. The neck has to be rather wide and a fourth of the stitches must be allotted for the sleeves so that the sweater doesn't sit too high up under the chin. This model is comfortable and easy to put on because you don't need to worry about which side is the back or front. However, I rather quickly decided to knit the back a little longer than the front. In spite of other factors, it fits more comfortably.

A Sweater, Jacket, Cardigan, or Vest

Casting On

Cast on for the neck with a 40 cm/16 inch circular needle. Eventually, you can change to an 80 cm/32 inch circular needle when the short one has too many stitches. Sometimes, I switch to a 60 cm/24 inch needle after a few rows and then to the longer needle.

How many stitches you cast on depends on how wide you want the neck to be. For a sweater, you must have as many stitches as necessary so that it will go over your head. If you want a wider neck, you need to add more stitches.

Be sure and add in extra stitches on the front if the garment will be cut up the center front for a jacket, cardigan, or vest.

Neckband

Knit a neckband without any increases. The width of the neckband can be only a few rows or as many as 15 rows. If you can't decide on how wide a neckband to make at the beginning, simply knit one row. When the garment is finished, pick out the cast-on yarn and knit a neckband.

Dividing into Sections

Now the garment needs to be divided into front, sleeve, back, sleeve. Place a marker on the needle between each section to make it easier to see where the increases for the raglan sleeve should be made. Next, decide how many stitches should be in each section.

If the sweater will be the same on both sides, you simply divide the piece into four equal sections. You do not need a turning row. The wide sleeves still leave enough stitches for a shaped neckline.

If the sweater will be knitted with a lower neck on the front and with rather wide sleeves, allow twice as many stitches for the front and back pieces as for the sleeves. In that case, because turned rows have to be worked a couple of times, a couple more increases will be needed for the sleeves at the back than on the front. You must take this into consideration at the very beginning and allow more stitches for the front than the back when dividing up stitches.

If the sweater will be knitted with a low neck on the front but not as wide sleeves, you can allow maybe only 10 stitches for the sleeves and the rest in equal amounts for the front and back pieces. But, the fewer stitches you have for the sleeves, the more turning rows you have to make on the front so that the sweater will not sit too high up on the neck.

I place the change of rows on a sweater at the raglan increases between the right sleeve and the front. The row ends, then, after the right sleeve and begins again on the front.

For a garment which will be cut, I place the row change at the center front. Do not work any patterning or turns on these 7 center front stitches.

Increasing for the Raglan Sleeves

Begin the increases for the raglan shaping on the first row after the neckband. The increases are worked at the beginning and end of each section, on each side of the marker. Usually, the relation between the stitch and row gauges is such that it works to increase on every row. Increase 8 stitches on every row or 2 stitches on each section. For thinner yarns, the sweater can become too wide if you increase on every row for the whole raglan. The last 8-10 increases can, therefore, be made every other row. That will fit a tall, thin body better.

If you want a fine, discreet raglan line, increase into the stitches nearest the marker. If you are knitting a striped pattern, it is easiest to increase this way; otherwise, you have to remember to twist the strands so that the colors will come out in the correct order.

If you want a more noticeable raglan line, knit a stitch on each side of the marker and increase in the stitches before/after these two knit stitches.

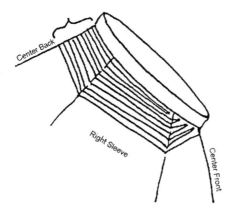

The picture shows how, looking at the center back, right sleeve, and center front, the turned rows raise the back.

In order for the back to be a little higher than the front, knit several rows back and forth. For details on how to make the turned/short rows, see Turned or Short Rows (p. 50).

Remember to make the increases for the raglan shaping at the same time as turning rows!

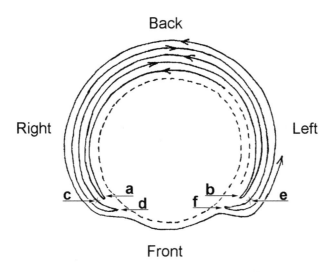

The picture shows the turns around the neck as seen from above.

A knit row is worked after the neckband, but not all the way around. The first turn is made at the sleeve and the rest of the front if the sleeves are knitted rather wide. If only a few stitches are allotted for the sleeves, all of the turns are made on the front.

Work to the right side (a) of the neck and make the "turning from right to wrong side."
Purl back on the right sleeve, back and left sleeve.
At the left side of the neck (b), make the "turning from wrong to right side."
Knit back over the left sleeve, back, right sleeve up to the turn made on the previous row (c).
Make the "working the stitches together on the right side."
Work a few more stitches and make a new "turning from right to wrong side." (d).
Purl back to the previous turn (e), make a "working the stitches together on the wrong side."
Continue, purling a few stitches, turn back again (f), etc.

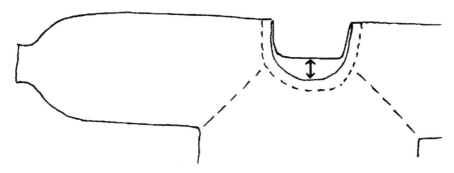

Make as many turned rows as necessary to create a large enough difference between the front and back pieces. How many turning rows are needed depends on the thickness of the yarn and how deep you want the neckline. How much spacing you need between the turns depends on how many turns you want to make. On a sweater with rather heavy yarn, I turn with 3 stitches between, 7-8 times on each side. For a thinner yarn, I can turn 10-12 times with 2 or 3 stitches between. If I want a rounder neckline, I turn 5-6 times with 2 stitches between and then a few times with 3 or 4 stitches between.

When all the turned rows have been completed, return to circular knitting. On that row, the final working together of the turned stitches, normally worked on the wrong side, should be made on the right side. Don't forget to switch the yarn-over and the next stitch before they are knitted together.

Working Each Section Separately

When you have knitted long enough for the correct depth of the armhole, the body and the sleeves have to be worked separately. Knit the front. Place the stitches for the left sleeve on a waste yarn. Cast on as many stitches as necessary under the sleeve. On a woman's sweater, the cast-on should be at least 5 cm/2 inches (see Casting on Several Stitches within the Work, p. 44). Knit the back. Place the stitches for the right sleeve on a waste yarn. Cast on the same number of stitches as for under the left sleeve.

Use a cotton or linen yarn for setting aside stitches. Wool can easily shift and can become fluffy and make an ugly color streak.

Body

Knit the body until desired length. Bind off with a single strand in the same way as for regular knitting but more tightly. Bind off with a new strand if the garment will be cut open.

Sleeves

Now it is time to complete the sleeves, one at a time. Slide the stitches from one sleeve from the waste yarn to a 40 cm/16 inch circular needle. Where the new stitches were cast on between the front and back, there is a row of loops. Pick up and knit in these loops so that you have 2 stitches more than you cast on. Begin and end by picking up and knitting a stitch at each end of the cast-on loops (see Picking Up and Knitting Stitches from Loops, p. 46). On the next row, decrease away these extra stitches on each side in order to avoid a hole which must otherwise be sewn together later on.

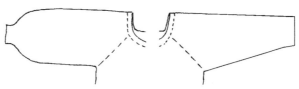

The sleeves can be knitted straight down with decrease rounds near the cuffs or with the decreases evenly divided down the length of the sleeve as for a drop sleeve (see An Example of How to Calculate the Numbers, p. 57).

For a puffed sleeve, add a bit of extra length to the sleeve. Knit until the sleeve feels almost long enough when you try it on. Then it will be time to begin decrease rows, each of which is made with several rows in between.

For example:
1st decrease row: Decrease 1, knit 4 or work a double decrease followed by 8 stitches.
2nd decrease row: Decrease 1, knit 3 or double decrease, knit 6
3rd decrease row: Decrease 1, knit 2 or double decrease, knit 4.

Try to place the decreases so that they make a pleasing completion of the pattern on the sleeve. Continue decreasing until you have the number of stitches you want for the cuff.

The cuffs are worked on double-pointed needles until the desired length. I have varied the cuffs from making only one chain path or a purl row before binding off up to 33 richly pattern rows.

Be sure and write down how you worked the first sleeve so that you can knit the other one exactly the same.

Finishing
Neatly weave in ends from the casting-on, binding off, and cast-on for the sleeves.

Now all that is left is to wash the garment.

INSTRUCTIONS

The following instructions should be considered as basic models. I have only given pattern suggestions for the mittens.

Sweaters, cardigans, and skirts are so flexible in their fit that it is difficult to assign a more exact sizing than Medium. However, that can also fit as a large Small and a small Large with a little adjustment in, for example, the length of the sleeves.

Yarn and Gauge

The instructions are designed for the use of a Z-plied blanket yarn number 6/2. The yarn can be ordered from Firma Krokmaskan (see copyright page) in natural white, light grey, dark grey, and in about 25 different colors.

I use needles size 3 mm (in between U.S. sizes 2 and 3) for all the patterns except for the mittens, with a *gauge of 3.6 stitches and 3.2 rows per centimeter (approximately 9 stitches and 8 rows per inch).*

For the mittens, I use needles 2.5 mm (in between U. S. sizes 1 and 2), with a *gauge of 3.8 stitches and 3.4 rows per centimeter (approximately 9.5 stitches and 8.5 rows per inch).*

If you knit more loosely, you should go down a half mm size or one U.S. size for the needles. If you knit too loosely, you will lose some of the character of the technique and the curled stitches will be rather untidy.

If you knit too tightly but feel comfortable with that, it is better to add more stitches and rows than to work on larger needles. Two-end knitting can never be too tight.

SWEATER Loose Fit

Yarn: 10 x 100 grams (approximately 35 ounces)
Needles: 40 and 80 cm (16 and 32 inch) circular and a 60 cm/24 inch
        circular if desired. Double-pointed needles for the cuffs.
Notions: 4 small markers

Cast on 180 stitches with cast-on method 2 and knit a neckband.
Suggestion for a nice border worked over 9 rows: Work 1 knit row, 1 purl
row, 2 knit, a chain path (= 2 hook stitch rows), 2 knit and 1 purl row. Finish
the cuffs and lower edge with the same band.
On the first row after the neckband, mark off the sections by placing
markers.
Divide as follows: 64 stitches for the front, 30 each for the sleeves, and 56
for the back.

Work 9 short rows with 4 stitches between each turning.
Make the first 2 turns on the sleeves and turn 7 times more on each side of
the front.
Remember that the increases for the raglan shaping must be made at the
same time.
Place the pattern in a pleasing manner on each piece.

Increase for the raglan shaping on every row until you have 684 stitches on
the needle. If you want a smaller size, finish before you have reached that
number. If you want a larger size for the sweater, work a few extra rows and
increase a few more stitches.
Work one row without increasing.
Now the work is ready to be divided into front, back, and sleeve sections.
Divide it so that you have 192 stitches each for the front and back and 150
stitches for each sleeve. That means that the stitches from the raglan shaping
go onto the body pieces.
Place the stitches for the sleeves onto a waste yarn; cast on 20 new stitches
at each underarm.

Work body until desired length. Usually about 140 rows counted down from
the underarm are enough for a regular sweater. Of course, you can decide for
yourself if the sweater should be waist- or knee-length. Bind off tightly,
using a single strand.

Sleeves: Slip the sleeve stitches from the waste yarn to a 40 cm/16 inch
circular needle.
Pick up and knit 22 stitches from the loops of the cast-on between the body
sections.
On the first row, decrease one stitch at each end of the picked up and knitted
stitches.

For puffy sleeves, you should be able to decrease for the cuffs about 130
rows from the underarm, but try on the sweater first. When you have the
sweater on, the sleeves should feel as if they are almost to the point where
the decreasing for the cuffs should begin. Decrease until at least 76 stitches
remain, knit the cuffs on double-pointed needles, making the cuffs as long as
you desire. Bind off tightly.

For drop shoulder sleeves, work about 20 rows without any decreasing.
Then decrease 2 stitches on every 3rd row 35-40 times (or until you have
about 90 stitches left), depending on how wide and long you want the
sleeves to be. Bind off tightly.
Work the other sleeve in the same way.

Weave in ends and wash the sweater.

SWEATER Fitted

Yarn: 9-10 x 100 grams (approximately 32-35 ounces)
Needles: 40 and 80 cm (16 and 32 inch) circular and a 60 cm/24 inch
      circular if desired. Double-pointed needles for the cuffs.
Notions: 4 small markers

Cast on 160 stitches with cast-on method 2 and knit a neckband.
On the first row after the neckband, mark off the sections by placing
markers.
Divide as follows: 70 stitches each for the front and back and 10 each for the
sleeves.

Work 8 short rows with 3 stitches between each turn and then 1 row with 4
stitches between. All of the turns are made on the front piece.
Remember that the increases for the raglan shaping must be made at the
same time.
Place the pattern in a pleasing manner on each piece.

Increase for the raglan shaping on every row until you have 520 stitches on
the needle. Then increase for the raglan shaping every other row until you
have a total of 616 stitches.
Work one row without increasing.
Now the work is ready to be divided into front, back, and sleeve sections.
Divide it so that you have 184 stitches each for the front and back and 124
stitches for each sleeve.
Place the stitches for the sleeves onto a waste yarn; cast on 20 new stitches
at each underarm.

Work body until desired length.
Bind off tightly, using a single strand.

Sleeves: Slip the sleeve stitches from the waste yarn to a 40 cm/16 inch
circular needle.
Pick up and knit 22 stitches from the loops of the cast-on between the body
sections.
On the first row, decrease one stitch at each end of the picked up and knitted
stitches.

For puffy sleeves, you should be able to decrease for the cuffs about 130
rows from the underarm, but try on the sweater first. When you have the
sweater on, the sleeves should feel as if they are almost to the point where
the decreasing for the cuffs should begin. Decrease until at least 76 stitches
remain, knit the cuffs on double-pointed needles, making the cuffs as long as
you desire. Bind off tightly, using a single strand.
Work the other sleeve in the same way.

Weave in ends and wash the sweater.

SWEATER Yoke Model

Yarn: 10 x 100 grams (approximately 35 ounces)
Needles: 40 and 80 cm (16 and 32 inch) circular and a 60 cm/24 inch
        circular if desired. Double-pointed needles for the cuffs.
Notions: 8 small markers in one color and 2 in another color.

Cast on 160 stitches with cast-on method 2 and knit a neckband.
On the first row after the neckband, divide the work into 8 sections. Place markers in one color at each section so you can see in which area the increases for the yoke will be made.
Place a marker in another color at each side of the front to mark where the short rows for the neckline will be made. There should be about 60 stitches between these markers.

Work 9 short rows with 2 stitches between each turn.
Remember that the increases for the yoke must be made at the same time with 8 stitches on every row or 16 stitches on every other row until you have a total of 600 stitches on the needle. The increases on the front should be divided among the other pieces when the first turned row is worked. After that, increase every other row until you have 640 stitches on the needle. All of the increases are made *unevenly* divided on every eighth part. They should not be straight over one another.
Place the pattern so that it won't be too difficult to make the increases. It is easy and pretty to use only a few rows of hook stitch.

Work one row without increasing.
Now the work is ready to be divided into front, back, and sleeve sections. Divide it so that you have 190 stitches each for the front and back and 130 stitches for each sleeve. Place the stitches for the sleeves onto a waste yarn; cast on 20 new stitches at each underarm.

In order for a yoke sweater to fit well, the material which is "lost" at the underarm is added as a dart on both the front and back. You should work at least 5 short rows at each underarm. Begin at the first underarm by knitting 15 stitches past the cast-on, turn and purl back these 15 stitches, past the cast-on and 15 stitches more. Turn again. Continue working back and forth and work 15 stitches more each time so that you are reaching the center of the front and back pieces. Work the turns as you did for the neckline. Work darts at the other underarm.
Work body until desired length. Bind off tightly with a single strand.

Sleeves: Slip the sleeve stitches from the waste yarn to a 40 cm/16 inch circular needle.
Pick up and knit 22 stitches from the loops of the cast-on between the body sections.
On the first row, decrease one stitch at each end of the picked up and knitted stitches.
For drop shoulder sleeves: after about 20 rows without decreasing, decrease 2 stitches on every 3rd row until 90-100 stitches remain.
For puffy sleeves with a cuff, try on the sweater when you think the sleeves are long enough. When you have the sweater on, the sleeves should feel as if they are almost to the point where the decreasing for the cuffs should begin. Decrease until 76 stitches remain for the cuffs. Work the other sleeve in the same way.

Weave in ends and wash the sweater.

CARDIGAN/JACKET

Yarn: 8-10 x 100 grams (28-35 ounces), depending on garment length
Needles: 40 and 80 cm (16 and 32 inch) circular and a 60 cm/24 inch
      circular if desired. Double-pointed needles for the cuffs.
Notions: 5 small markers; buttons if desired.

Cast on 169 stitches with cast-on method 2 and knit a neckband of not more than 8-10 rows.
Divide for the sections, placing markers. Position the row change at center front.
Divide as follows: 67 stitches for the front (place a marker at the center front to indicate the cutting line), 24 stitches each for the sleeves, and 54 stitches for the back.
Work turned rows and remember to work the increases for the raglan shaping at the same time. The first 2 short rows are made on the sleeves, so, on the first row, there should not be any increases for the raglan on the front and only on one side of the sleeve. Make 10 turns with 2 stitches between and 2 turns with 4 stitches between on each side of the front.

Decide on a pattern and where it should begin. Place it pleasingly, considering how it will look on each side of the front. Do not work any patterning over the 7 stitches at the center front or over the increase lines for the raglan shaping.

Increase for the raglan shaping until there are 699 stitches on the needle. Work a row without increasing.
Divide the work into front, back, and sleeve sections. Divide as follows: 199 stitches for the front, 192 for the back, and 154 each for the sleeves. Place the stitches for the sleeves onto a waste yarn; cast on 20 new stitches at each underarm.

Work body until desired length. For a jacket, that could be 90 rows after the division and for a cardigan, you might want 130 rows after the underarm. Cut yarns and bind off with another strand. Begin and end binding off at center front, first placing the center stitch (cutting line) on a safety pin. This prevents accidental cutting of the bind-off strand.

Sleeves: Slip the sleeve stitches from the waste yarn to a 40 cm/16 inch circular needle. Pick up and knit 22 stitches from the loops of the cast-on between the body sections. On the first row, decrease one stitch at each end of the picked up and knitted stitches.
For drop shoulder sleeves: after about 20 rows without decreasing, decrease 2 stitches on every 3rd row until 90-100 stitches remain.
For puffy sleeves with a cuff, try on the sweater when you think the sleeves are long enough. When you have the sweater on, the sleeves should feel as if they are almost to the point where the decreasing for the cuffs should begin. Decrease until 76 stitches remain for the cuffs. Work the other sleeve in the same way.

Wash the cardigan before you continue so that it will be smooth and fine. Reinforce the stitches with a seam on each side of the stitch you will cut at the front; cut.
Pick up and knit stitches for the front band with an 80 cm/32 inch circular needle. You can use a straight needle but will be easier with a circular needle. It should be sufficient to pick up 2 stitches for every 3 rows. If you have knitted the cardigan a total of 180 rows long, you should have 120 stitches for the front band. Work in regular, single strand knitting to desired width. Purl one row for the turn and then work the same number of rows as before the turn. Bind off loosely because you have just used regular knitting. Neatly sew down the facing of the band on the wrong side.
Both front bands are worked alike but remember to make the buttonholes on one side if you desire.

FAKE TURTLENECK or DICKEY

If you don't dare begin knitting a sweater all at once, it would be good to begin practicing the turned rows on a fake turtleneck. At the same time, try out a pattern motif you like.

Cast on as many stitches as needed so that the turtleneck will go over your head. The number of cm/inches x the stitch gauge = the number of stitches.

This will go over your head if you remember to take your glasses off first!

Yarn: 100 grams (3.5 ounces)
Needles: 40 cm/16 inch circular needle
Notions: 4 small markers

Cast on 152 stitches with cast-on method 2.
Knit a neckband of at least 5 cm/2 inches.
Divide the piece by placing small markers on the needle so that the "front" and "back" each have 50 stitches and each "sleeve" 26 stitches.
Begin to increase for the raglan shaping on each side of the small markers (= 8 stitches increased on each row) at the same time as the turned rows are begun.

Because most people like a turtleneck rather high up on the neck, turning 7 times on each side of the front with 3 stitches between is recommended. Work as follows:
Knit 2 stitches in on the front and make a "turning from the right to wrong side."
Purl back until 2 stitches in on the other side of the front.
Make the "turning from wrong to right side."
Knit back to the first turning.
Make the "working together on the right side." Knit the first yarn-over with the next stitch.
Knit 3 more stitches and turn again from right to wrong side.
Purl to the first turning on that side.
Make "working together on the wrong side." Switch the position of the yarn-over and the next stitch and purl them together.
Purl 3 more stitches and turn again. Continue in the same way.

Continue increasing for the raglan shaping when the turned rows are completed with 8 stitches on every row until the back measures 15 cm/6 inches. Bind off sleeves and back with a new strand.

The front is still too short, so you need to knit a few more rows, working back and forth. Decrease 1 stitch at each side on every row until the piece is long enough.
Bind off and weave in ends.

VEST

Yarn: 7 x 100 grams (approximately 25 ounces)
Needles: 40 and 80 cm (16 and 32 inch) circular
Notions: 5 small markers

Cast on 163 stitches with cast-on method 1.
Do not knit a neckband; instead, knit 1 row after the cast-on. The neck edge is worked last after the vest front has been cut open and the front bands knitted on.
Divide the sections as follows by placing markers: 77 stitches for the front, placing a little marker at the center front to mark the cutting line. Allot 10 stitches each for the sleeves and 64 stitches for the back.
Work 10 short rows with 2 stitches between each turning on the front.
Remember to work the increases for the raglan shaping at the same time.

Place the pattern you've chosen so it is centered at the back and on each side of the center front. Remember not to work any patterning over the 7 stitches at the center front.

Increase for the raglan shaping on every row until there are 527 stitches on the needle and then on every other row until there are 623 stitches.
Work one row without increasing.
Divide the work for front, back, and sleeves: 191 stitches for the front, 184 stitches for the back and 124 stitches each for the sleeves.
Cast on 20 new stitches at each underarm and knit the body to desired length.
Cut yarn and bind off with a new strand. Begin and end binding off at the center front, first setting aside the center cutting line stitch onto a safety pin to avoid cutting the binding off.

Transfer the stitches for sleeves onto a 40 cm (16 inch) circular needle for finishing.
Knit 1 row, decreasing 12 stitches evenly divided over the row.
Finish with 1 chain path (= 2 hook rows) and one knit row.
Bind off tightly using a single strand.

Wash the garment before you continue so that it will be smooth and fine.
Reinforce the stitches with a seam on each side of the cutting line on the front; cut.
Pick up and knit stitches for the front band on an 80 cm (32 inch) circular needle. It should be sufficient to pick up 2 stitches for every 3 rows. Work in regular single strand knitting until desired width. Purl one row for the turning and then work the same number of rows as before the turning row. Bind off loosely because you have just worked regular knitting. Sew down edging neatly on wrong side. Both front edges should be worked alike but remember to make buttonholes on one side if you so desire.

Remove the cast-on thread, pick up the stitches and make a neck band in two-end knitting.

If you want a V-neck vest, cut a corner on each side of the front edge. Of course, the stitches should be secured with a seam first. Remove the cast-on thread at the neck and pick up and knit stitches around the whole edging. An 80 cm/32 inch circular needle should be long enough for all the stitches. Work a continuous piece in regular single strand knitting to desired width. Purl one row for the turning and then work the same number of rows as before the turning row; bind off loosely. Turn the edging and sew neatly to the wrong side.

SILK BLOUSE

Yarn: Schappe silk number 248 (4000 m/kg) from Atelje Git, Smedsbol, 642 00 Flen, Sweden.
Amount: 8 x 100 grams (approximately 28 ounces).
Needles. 40 and 80 cm (16 and 32 inch) circular needles size 2 mm/U.S. 0. Double ponted needles for sleeve cuffs.
Notions: 4 small markers
Gauge: 4.4 stitches and 4.6 rows per centimeter or 11 stitches and 11.5 rows per inch
Size: 42-44 (large)

Cast on 200 stitches with cast-on method 2 and knit a neckband.

On the first row after the neckband, place markers between the sections.
Divide as follows: 56 stitches for the front, 42 each for the sleeves, and 60 for the back.
Knit 10 short rows with 4 stitches between each turning.
Make the first 3 turns on the sleeves and then turn 7 times on each side of the front.
Remember to increase for the raglan shaping at the same time as working turned rows.

Throughout, increase for the raglan every row until you have 796 stitches on the needle.
Knit one row without increasing.
Divide the work into front – back – and sleeves.
Divide as follows: 210 stitches each for the front and back and 188 stitches each for the sleeves. That means that the stitches from the raglan shaping line will be on the body sections. Place the sleeve stitches on a waste yarn.
Cast on 28 new stitches at each underarm. Knit the body until desired length.
Bind off very tightly with only a single strand.

Sleeves: Place the stitches from the waste yarn onto a 40 cm/16 inch circular needle.
Pick up and knit 30 stitches from the cast-on row between the body sections.
On the first row, decrease one stitch at each side of the underarm cast-on row.
Knit about 170 rows. When the blouse is on, the sleeves should feel as if they are almost long enough before the decreases are begun.
Decrease until 92 stitches remain; knit the cuffs on double-pointed needles over about 20 rows. Finish and bind off tightly within only a single strand.

Be sure and write down what you've done on the first sleeve so that you can knit the other exactly alike.

Weave in ends and wash blouse.

SKIRT   Straight, Fitted Model

Yarn: 4-5 x 100 grams (approximately 14-18 ounces)
Needles: 80 cm/32 inch circular needle
Notions: 2 cm/1 inch wide waistband elastic

Cast on 312 stitches with cast-on method 1.
Work the waistband facing with 12 knit rows, one purl row for turning and 12 more knit rows.
Remove cast-on thread. Turn piece so that the wrong side is facing out. Pick up a loop from the cast-on edge and knit it together with a stitch on the needle. Continue around, leaving a 3-4 cm/1.25-1.5 inch opening so that you can insert the waistband elastic.

Increase 20 stitches evenly divided over the first row.

Then, increase 2 stitches on each side on every 3rd row, 14 times. When these have increases have been made, you should have 388 stitches on the needle.

Continue knitting the skirt straight down until desired length. Bind off tightly using only a single strand. A hem is not necessary.

Insert the elastic into the facing. Sew the opening loosely or with a thread in a contrasting color that it is easy to remove if the elastic needs to be changed later on.

Wash and centrifuge (spin) the skirt. Lay the skirt on a table and hit and pound it flat with your fists and then hang it up to dry on a skirt hanger.

SKIRT   Very Full

Yarn: 8-9 x 100 grams (28-32 ounces)
Needles: 80 cm/32 inch circular needle
Notions: 2 cm/1 inch wide waistband elastic

Cast on 312 stitches with cast-on method 1.
Work the waistband facing with 12 knit rows, one purl row for turning and 12 more knit rows.
Remove cast-on thread. Turn piece so that the wrong side is facing out. Pick up a loop from the cast-on edge and knit it together with a stitch on the needle. Continue around, leaving a 3-4 cm/1.25-1.5 inch opening so that you can insert the waistband elastic.

Increase 16 stitches evenly divided over the first row.
Then, increase 2 stitches on each side every 3rd row, 14 times.
Knit 5 rows without increasing.

You now have 384 stitches on the needle.
Now, a large increase will be made in the width of the skirt by increasing on just one row.
Make an increase in every 5th stitch around.
Knit 4 rows without increasing.
Increase in every 6th stitch around.
Knit 4 rows without increasing.
Increase in every 7th stitch around.
Knit 4 rows without increasing.
Increase in every 8th stitch around.
Knit 4 rows without increasing.
Increase in every 9th stitch around.
Knit 4 rows without increasing.
Increase in every 10th stitch around.

Knit the skirt until desire length which can be anything between short-short to ankle length. 250 rows after the facing is a comfortable length for many.
It is nice to finish the lower edge with a little border. A hem is not needed.
Bind off tightly using only a single strand.

Insert the elastic into the facing. Sew the opening loosely or with a thread in a contrasting color that it is easy to remove if the elastic needs to be changed later on.

Wash and centrifuge (spin) the skirt. Lay the skirt on a table and hit and pound it flat with your fists and then hang it up to dry on a skirt hanger.

SKIRT   A-Line

Yarn: 9 x 100 grams (32 ounces)
Needles: 80 cm/32 inch circular needle
Notions: 2 cm/1 inch wide waistband elastic; 6 small markers

Cast on 316 stitches with cast-on method 1.
Work the waistband facing with 12 knit rows, one purl row for turning and 12 more knit rows.
Remove cast-on thread. Turn piece so that the wrong side is facing out. Pick up a loop from the cast-on edge and knit it together with a stitch on the needle. Continue around, leaving a 3-4 cm/1.25-1.5 inch opening so that you can insert the waistband elastic.

Increase 20 stitches evenly divided over the first row.

Place markers dividing the skirt into 6 sections.
Divide as follows: 84 stitches each for front and back and 42 stitches each for panels, two on each side.
Place the first marker at the beginning of the row and knit 42 stitches for the first side panel; place marker; knit 84 stitches; place marker; 42 stitches; place marker; 42 stitches, place marker; 84 stitches; place marker, and 42 stitches.
Now the positions for the increases have been marked.

Increase 1 stitch on each side of each marker every 5th row, 40-50 times or until the skirt is desired length. Then bind off tightly, using only a single strand.

Insert the elastic into the facing. Sew the opening loosely or with a thread in a contrasting color that it is easy to remove if the elastic needs to be changed later on.

Wash and centrifuge (spin) the skirt. Lay the skirt on a table and hit and pound it flat with your fists and then hang it up to dry on a skirt hanger.

MITTENS   Single Color with a Straight Thumb

Yarn: 100 grams (3 ½ ounces), somewhat more for men's size
Needles: set of 5 double-pointed needles
Notions: A linen or cotton thread for holding thumb stitches
Size: Women's (Men's)

Cast on 72 (88) stitches
Hand: Divide stitches 18 (22) onto each of the 4 needles.
Knit 1 1/2 rows (over 6 needles) in order to be able to make a tassel at the
outside of the hand with the cast-on strands and so that the row changes will
be at the thumb. (The row changes could also be centered on the palm.)
Begin working the pattern you have chosen. On the cuff, the pattern is
knitted around. Do not work the pattern on the palm.

Work about 40 (44) rows before the thumb.
Using a waste yarn, knit 16 (20) stitches for the thumbhole. Move these
stitches back to the left needle and knit them again with the mitten yarn. Be
sure that the thumb lies on the correct side.

Work another 30 (34) rows or until the mitten reaches the little finger before
beginning the decreases for the top shaping at each side.

Band decreases on every row:
Needles 1 and 3: Knit a stitch. Knit 2 together in back loops.
Needles 2 and 4: Work until 3 stitches remain on needle. Knit 2 together in
front loops and knit the last stitch.

Decrease until 16 stitches remain; cut yarn; thread through remaining
stitches; draw tight and weave in end on inside.

Thumb: Remove waste yarn. Place stitches onto a needle and then pick up
the loops on the other side. You should have 32 (40) stitches for the thumb.
Work 20-22 (24-26) rows. Do not begin the decreases for the top until
reaching the top of the thumb.
Decrease until 12 stitches remain; finish as for top of hand.

Make a braid or cord with the cast-on strands or weave in ends on the inside.

Wash the mittens. Gently stretch the mittens in length and width so that they
are the correct size. Lay them flat on a hand towel. Press them with your
hand so that they are smooth and fine.

Hold the 4 strands apart from each other.

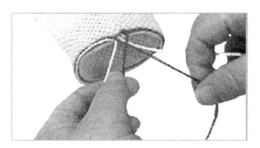

Cross the cast-on extra strand over the strands
you knitted with.

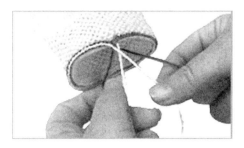

Continue crossing the strands over each other
until the braid is desired length.

Or a cord:

If you have used Z-plied yarn, twist the strands clockwise around each other,
two by two.
Then twist all four strands together counterclockwise.
If you have used S-plied yarn, twist in the opposite direction.

When the braid or cord is the desired length, finish with an overhand knot.

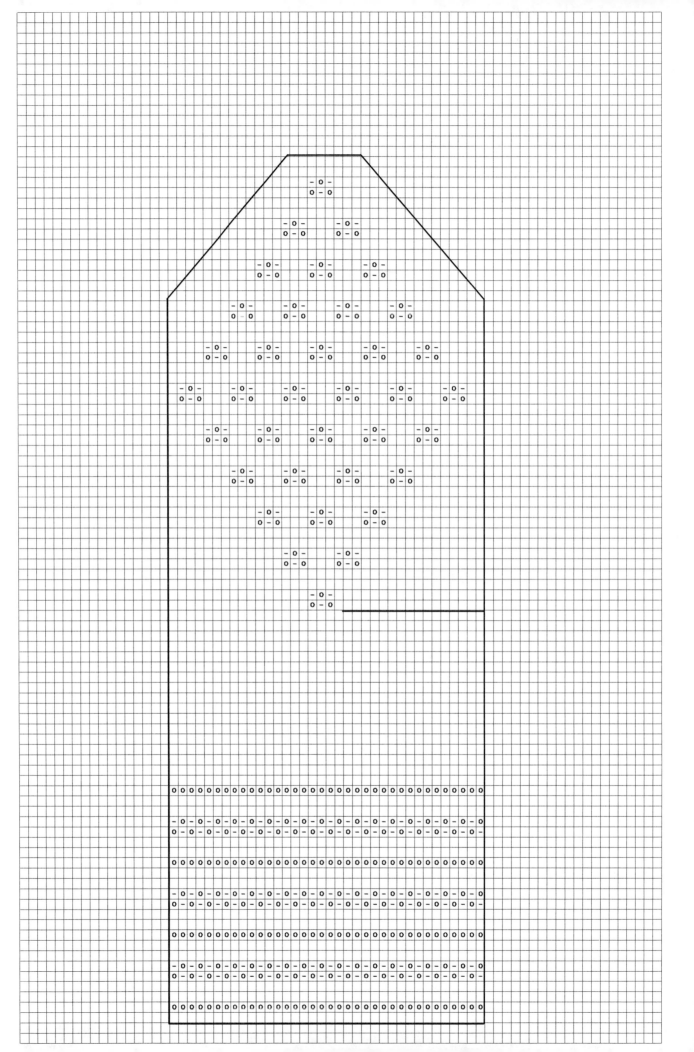

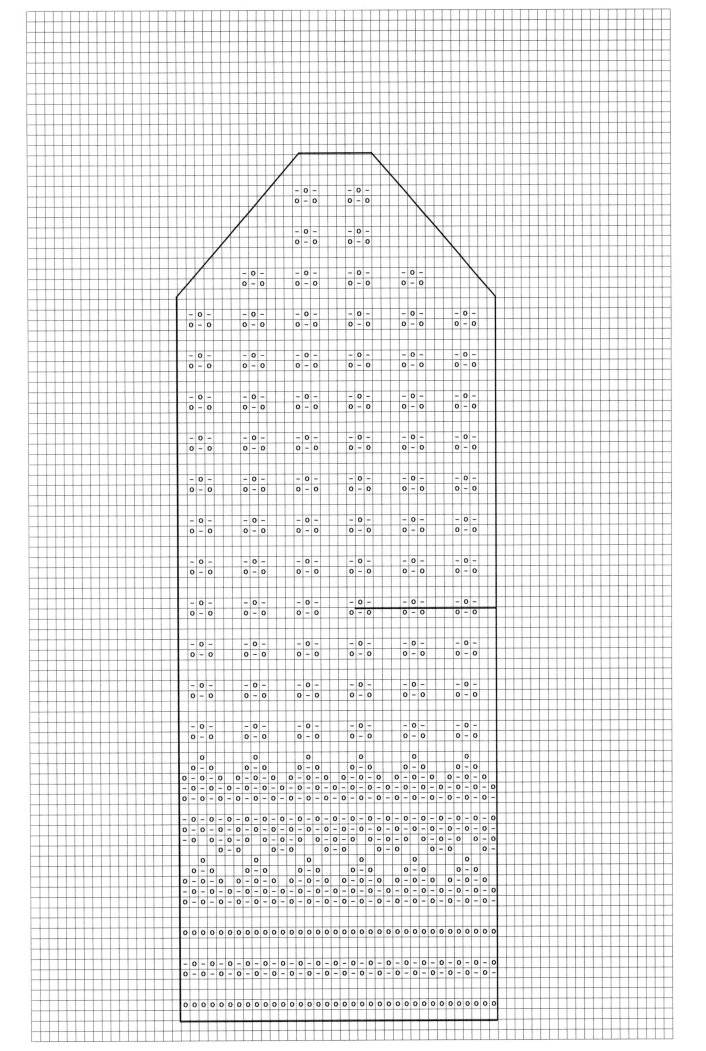

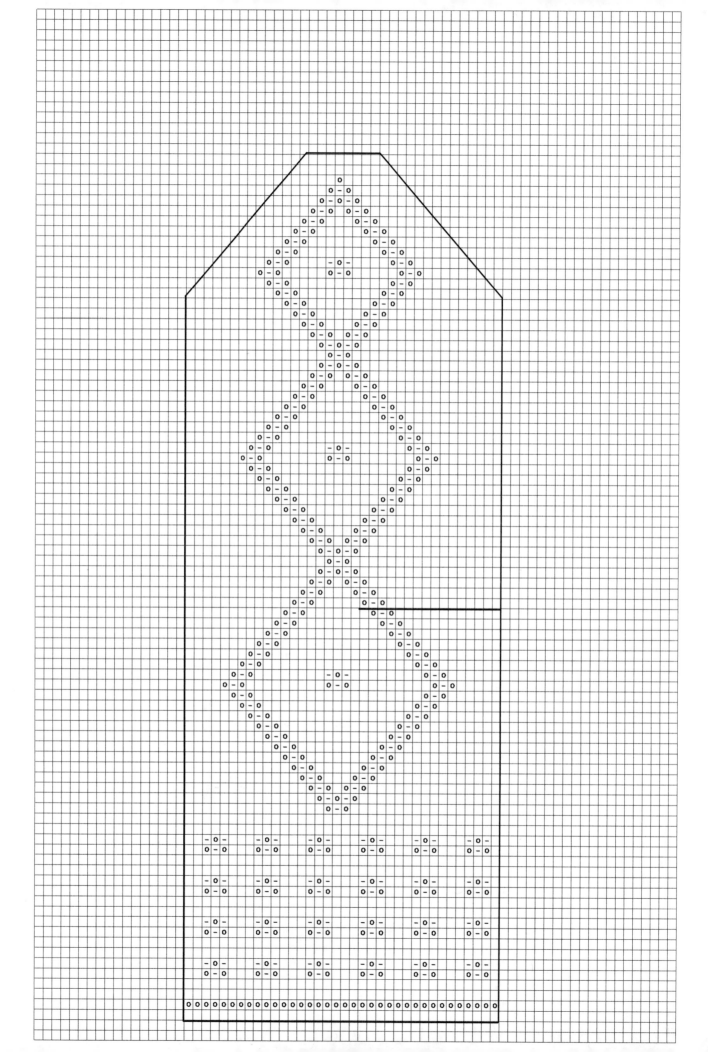

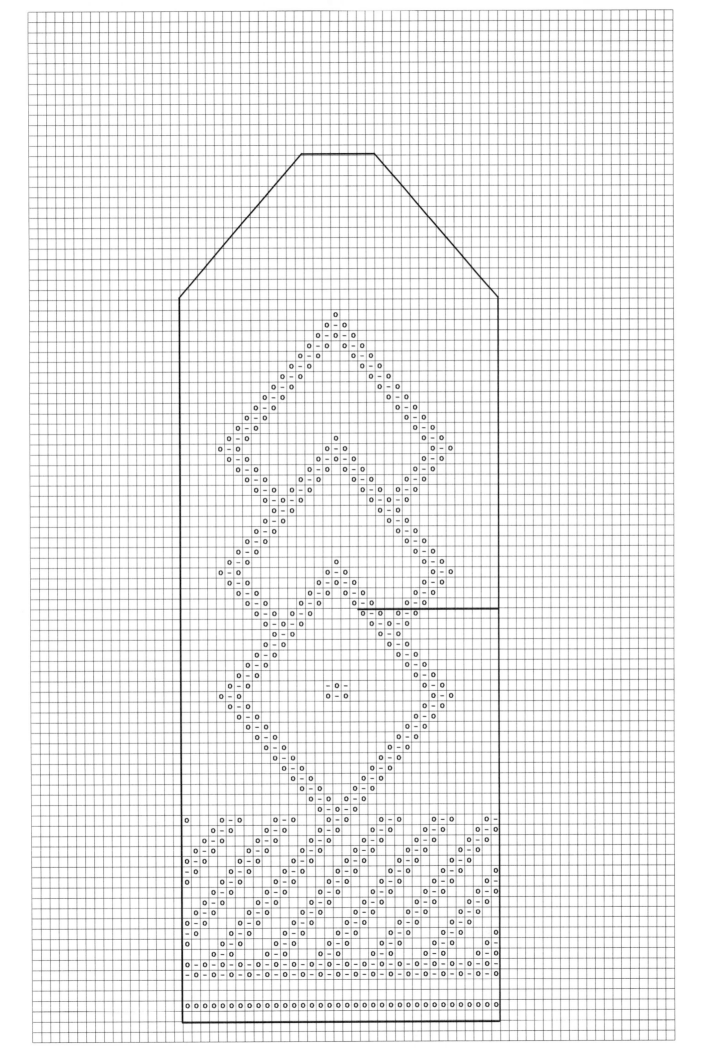

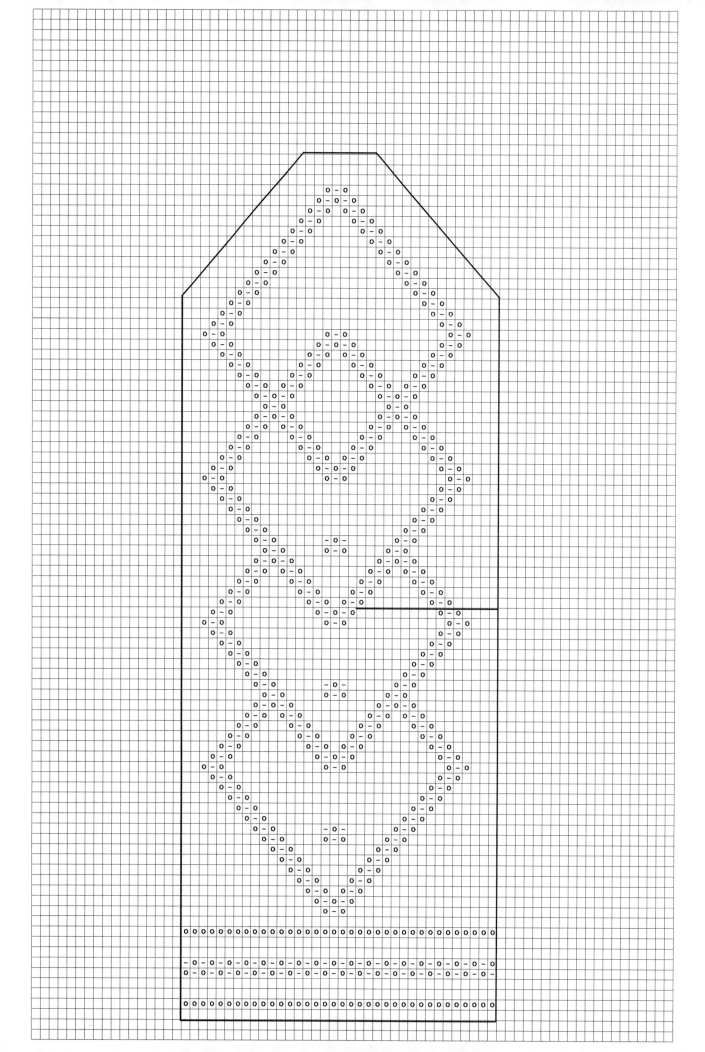

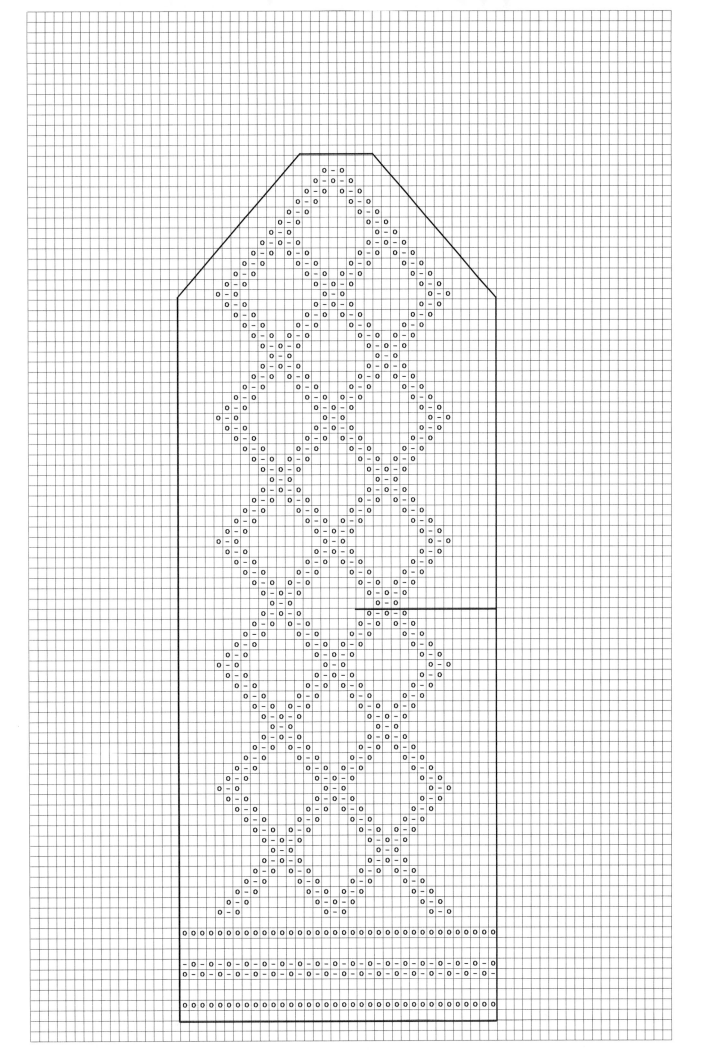

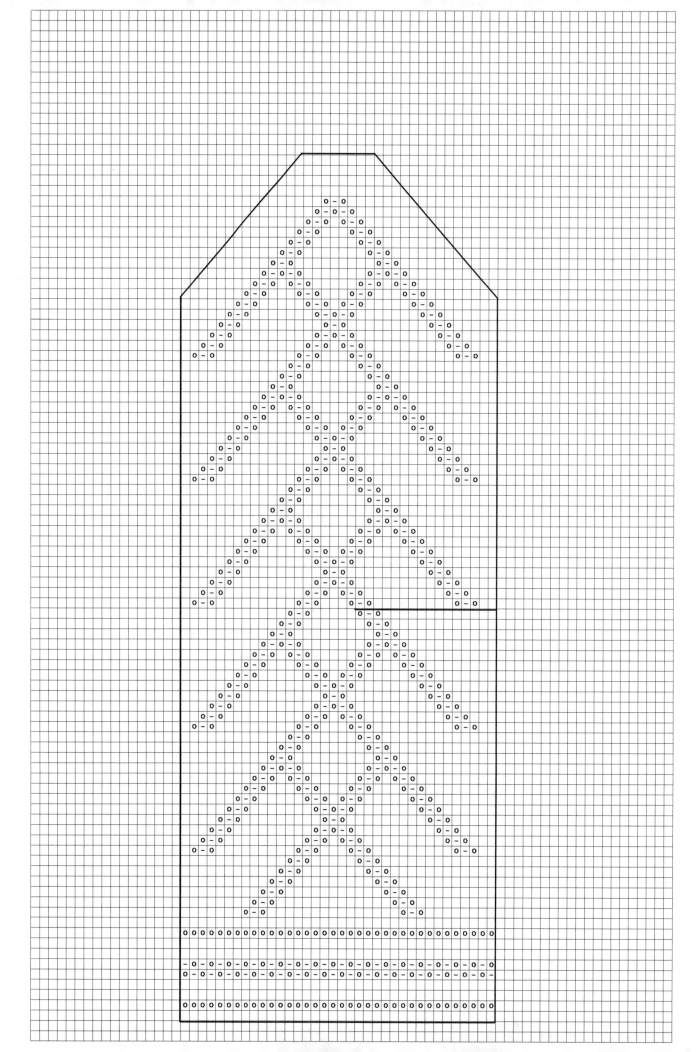

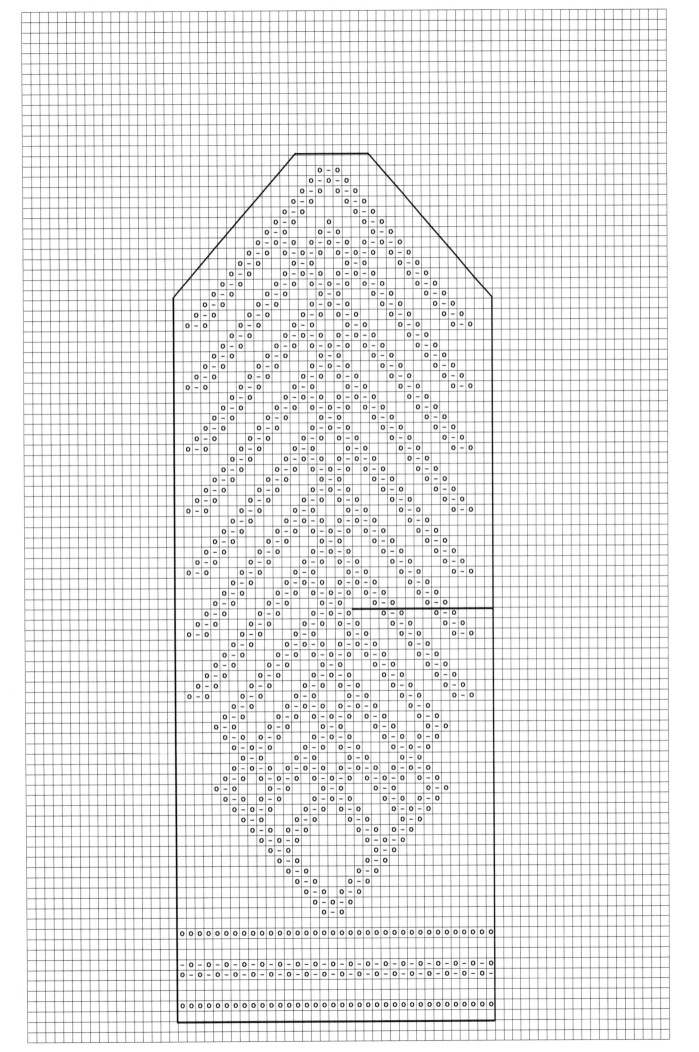

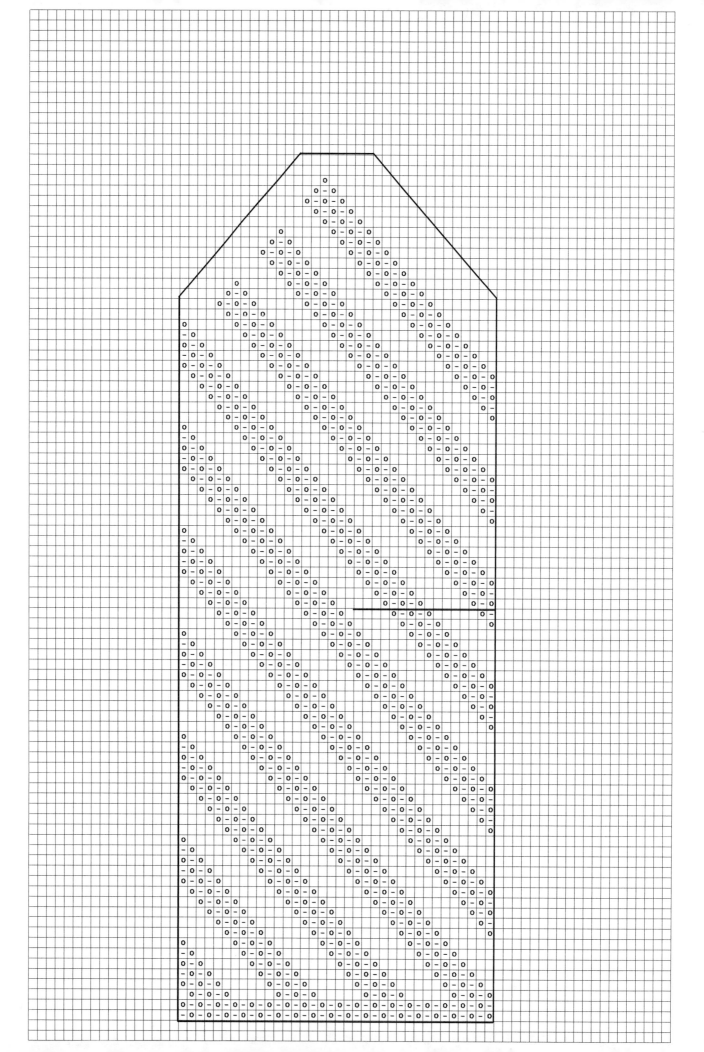

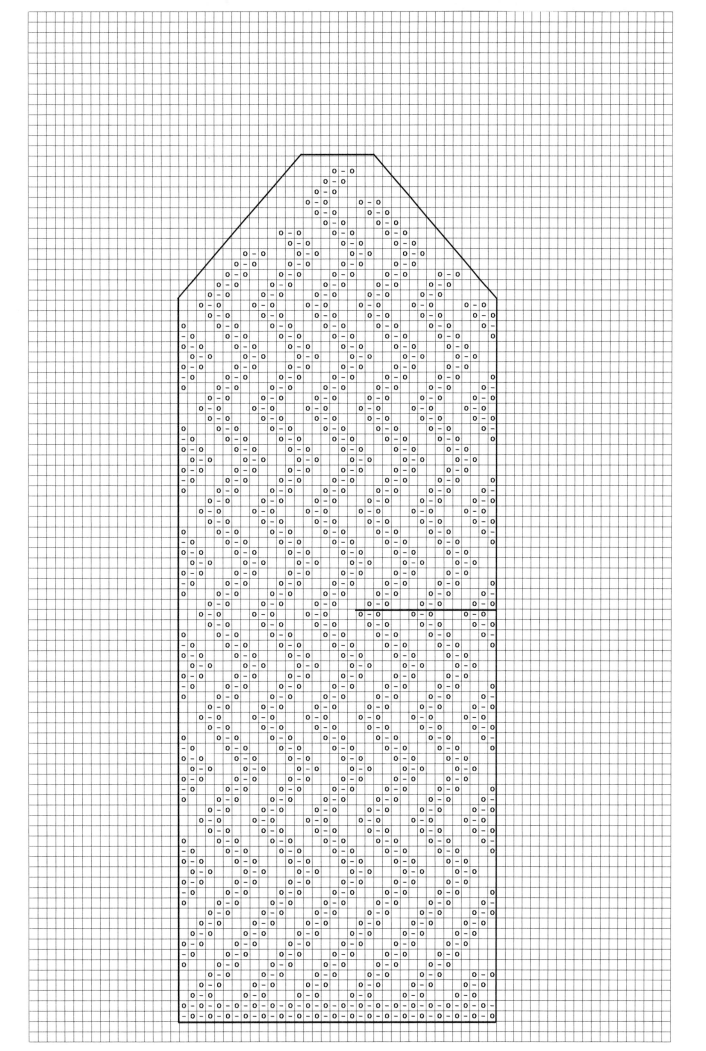

MITTENS   Striped with a Straight Thumb

Yarn: 100 grams (3 ½ ounces) total
Notions: A linen or cotton thread for holding the thumb stitches
Needles: set of 5 double-pointed needles

Wind one color onto a winding stick and then wind the other color on top so that you will automatically have striped knitting. Cast on 72 stitches. Work the first stitch with the light yarn on one mitten and the dark yarn on the other so that they will be mirror images of each other.
Hand: Divide stitches evenly onto 4 needles.
Knit 1 1/2 rows (over 6 needles) in order to be able to make a tassel at the outside of the hand with the cast-on strands and so that the row changes will be at the thumb.

Hook stitch pattern: Use the dark yarn for the purl stitches and the light for the knit stitches for a dark horizontal band. Use the light yarn for the purl stitches and the dark for the knit stitches for a light horizontal band.

Knit 40 rows or until desired length for cuff.

Using a waste yarn, knit 16 stitches for the thumb. Place these back onto the left needle and knit them again with pattern yarns. Be sure that the thumb lies on the correct side.

Knit about 30 rows or until the mitten reaches the top of the little finger before decreasing on each side.

Decreases are worked every row. On every other row, you will need to twist the threads an extra time so that you have the correct color for the next stitch:
Needles 1 and 3: Knit the first 2 stitches together through back loops.
Needles 2 and 4: Knit the last 2 stitches together through front loops.

Decrease until 16 stitches remain; cut yarn and thread through remaining stitches; pull tight and weave in end on inside.

Thumb: Pull out the waste yarn. Place the stitches from one side onto a needle and pick up new stitches from the loops on the other side. You should have 32 stitches for the thumb.
Knit 20-22 rows. Do not begin decreasing until you have reached the top of the thumb. Decrease until 12 stitches remain; cut yarn and thread through remaining stitches; pull tight and weave in end on inside.

Make a braid or cord with the cast-on strands or weave in ends on inside.

Wash the mittens: Gently stretch the mittens in length and width so that they are the correct size. Lay them flat on a hand towel. Press them with your hand so that they are smooth and fine.

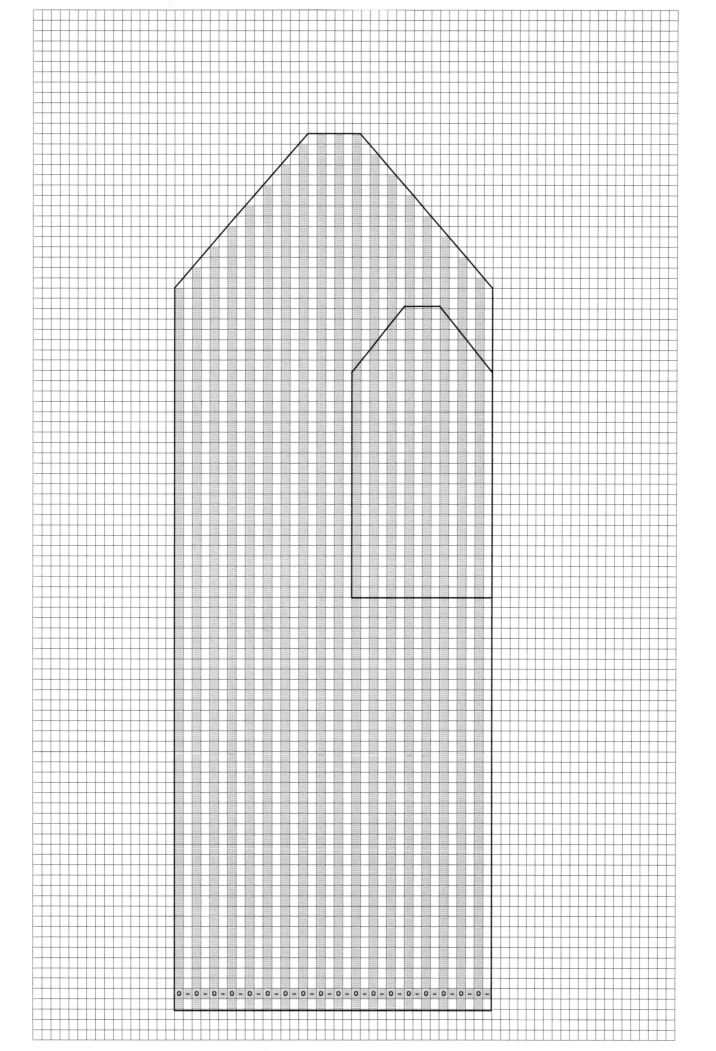

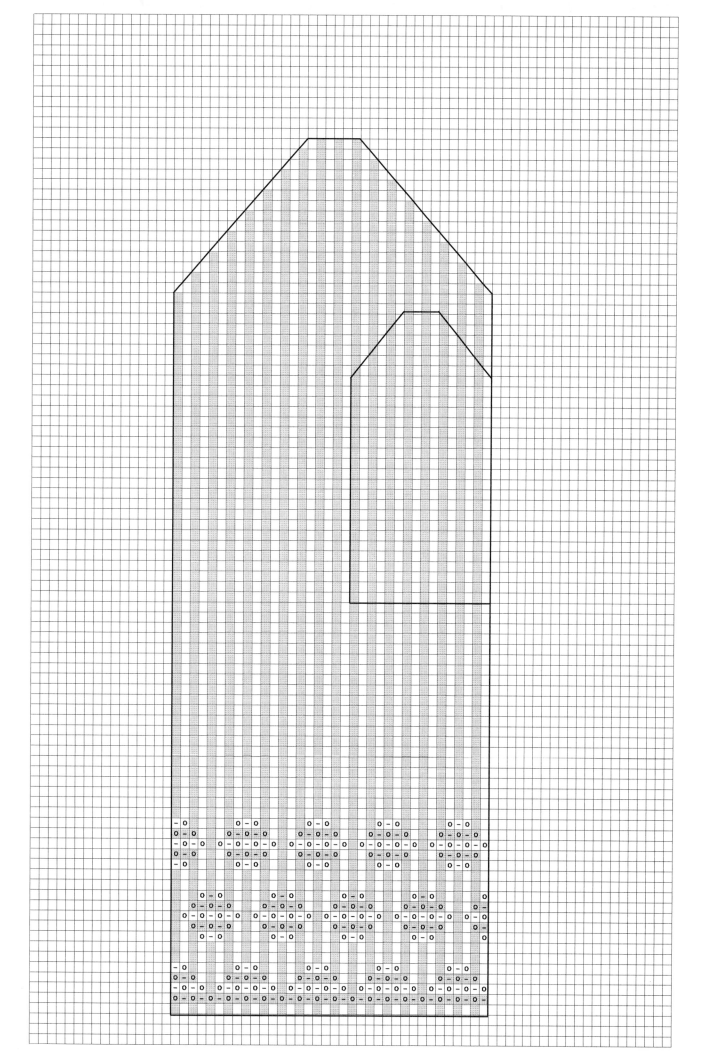

MITTENS   Single Color with a Gusset Thumb

Yarn: 100 grams (3 ½ ounces)
Needles: set of 5 double-pointed needles + an extra needle for thumb gusset stitches, if desired
Notions: A linen or cotton thread for holding thumb stitches

Cast on 71 stitches and divide them equally onto 4 needles. Knit 1 and a half rows (over 6 needles) in order to be able to make a tassel on the outside of the hand with the cast-on strands.
Cuff: Work a cuff with 15 rows of hook stitch. Increase 1 stitch.
Continue with hook stitches for the back of the hand, following the diagram. The palm is knitted in stockinette.

The thumb gusset can be shaped in many different ways. The increases can be centered on the thumb or made decoratively. A combination of straight thumb and a gusset increase on the hand's outside is also possible. Here is a suggestion for a symmetric increase on each side of the gusset.

Thumb gusset: The increases for this thumb gusset begin on the second row after the cuff. Be sure that the thumb lies in the right direction!
Increase 1 stitch on each side of the gusset on every other row, preferably placing the gusset a little bit in on the palm.
The left hand: knit until there are 4 stitches left on the needle. Increase in two stitches next to each other and then knit the last 2 stitches.
The next row is worked without increases. There are now 2 stitches between each increase stitch.
Work the next row until 6 stitches remain on the needle. Increase in 1 stitch, work 2 stitches, increase in a stitch and then work the last 2 stitches.
Now there are 4 stitches between each increase stitch.
Increase a total of 22 stitches.
On the *right hand's* needle 3, knit 2 stitches, increase in the next 2 stitches and knit the remaining 14 stitches.
(There will be many stitches on the "increase needle" so it is advised that you use a 6th needle to help.)

Hand: Work 1 row without any increases. Place the 22 stitches increased for the thumb onto a holder and cast on 12 new stitches.
Work 1 row. Form the 12 newly cast-on stitches into a little gusset by decreasing 2 stitches on each row of the first 6 rows.
Knit 25-30 rows or until the mitten covers the little finger before the shaping for the top is begun.

The "band" shaping is worked on every row:
Needles 1 and 3: Knit a stitch. Knit 2 together through back loops.
Needles 2 and 4: Work until 3 stitches remain on the row. Knit 2 together through front loops and knit the last stitch.
Continue decreasing in this manner until 12 stitches remain. Cut yarn and thread through remaining stitches. Weave in end on inside.

Thumb: Pick up the 22 stitches set aside for the thumb. Pick up and knit 14 new stitches where the 12 were cast on over the thumb. Use 4 of the 14 new stitches for a little gusset by decreasing 2 stitches each row on the first 2 rows.
32 stitches now remain for the thumb.
Work 16-20 rows. Do not begin top shaping until you have reached the top of the thumb. Decrease until 8 stitches remain, cut yarn and thread through remaining stitches. Weave in end on inside.

Make a braid or cord with the cast-on strands or weave in ends on the inside. Wash the mittens.Gently stretch the mittens in length and width so that they are the correct size. Lay them flat on a hand towel. Press them with your hand so that they are smooth and fine.

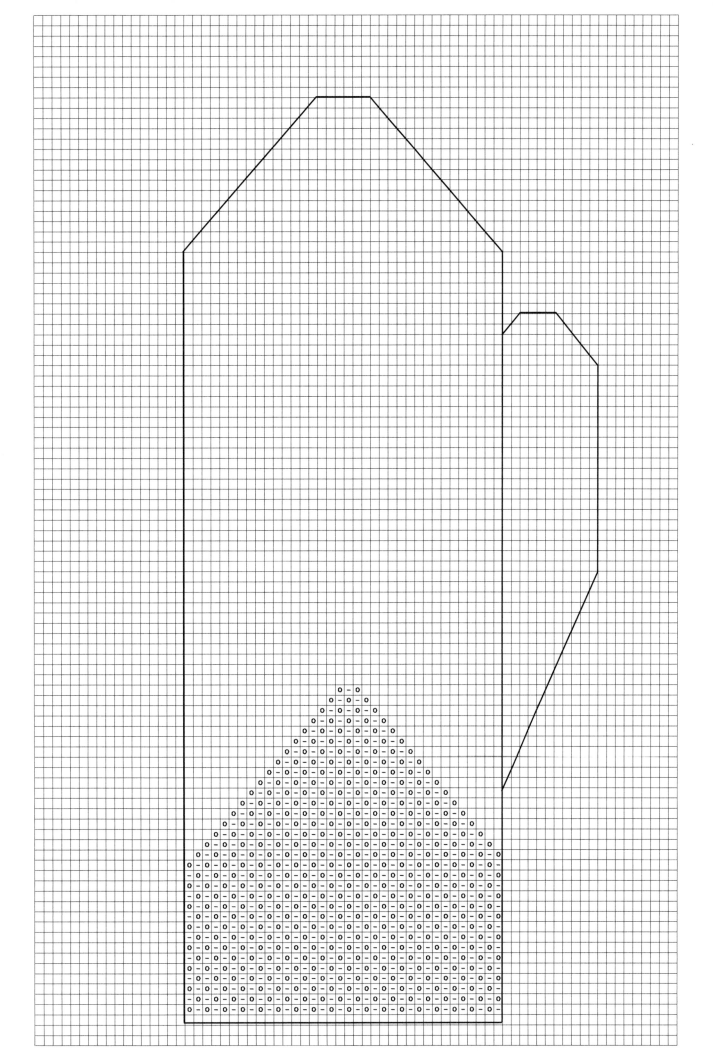

MITTENS   Striped with a Gusset Thumb

Yarn: 50 grams (1 3/4 ounce) of each color
Needles: set of 5 double-pointed needles + an extra needle for thumb gusset
stitches, if desired
Notions: A linen or cotton thread for holding thumb stitches

Wind one color on top of the other so that you will automatically have striped
knitting.
Cast on 72 stitches. Use the light yarn for the first stitch on one mitten and the
dark yarn to start the other so that the mittens will be mirror-imaged.
Place 18 stitches on each of the 4 needles.
Knit one and a half rows (over 6 needles) so that you can make a tassel at the
outside of the hand with the cast-on strands.
Cuff: Knit a cuff of 15 hook rows and shift colors at the inside of the hand on
every row.
When the purl stitches in the hook row are worked with the light strand, there will
be a light stripe and, with the dark strand, there will be a dark stripe. For the back
of the hand, continue working hook stitches following the chart. The palm is
worked in stockinette.

Thumb Gusset: Begin the increases for the gusset thumb on the second row after
completing the cuff. Be sure that the thumbs point in the right direction!
When you are knitting stripes, you must always remember to twist the strands an
extra time at every other increase or decrease so that each stitch is the correct
color.
Increase 1 stitch at each side of the gusset on every other row, placing the thumb
just in from the side of the hand, as follows:
Left hand: knit until 5 stitches remain on the needle. ncrease in one, knit one,
increase in one and then knit the last 2 stitches.
The next row is worked without increasing. There are now 3 stitches between
each increase stitch.
Knit the next row until 7 stitches remain on the needle. Increase in one stitch, knit
3, increase in one stitch and knit the last 2 stitches.
Now there are 5 stitches between each increase. Increase a total of 22 stitches.
Right hand: Knit 2 stitches, increase in one, knit one, increase in one stitch and
knit the last 13 stitches on the needle.
(If there are too many stitches on the "increase" needle, use a sixth needle.)

Hand: Knit 1 row without increasing. Place the 22 stitches which were increased
for the thumb onto a waste yarn and cast on 12 new stitches.
Knit 1 row. Form the 12 cast-on stitches into a little gusset by decreasing 2
stitches every row of the first 6 rows.
Knit 25-30 rows or until the mitten covers the little finger before beginning the
top shaping.
Top Shaping: Needles 1 and 3: Slip the first stitch knitwise, knit the second stitch
and pass slip stitch over.
Needles 2 and 4: Knit the last two stitches together.
Don't forget that, on every other row, you must twist the strands to the correct
color before the next stitch.
Work the decreases for the top shaping on every other row until 12 stitches
remain. Finish off.

Thumb: Place the 22 thumb stitches from the waste yarn onto a needle and knit
them. Pick up and knit 14 new stitches where the 12 stitches were cast on at the
thumbhole. Use 4 of these 14 stitches for a little gusset by decreasing 2 stitches
on each of the first 2 rows. There will be 32 stitches left for the thumb.
Knit 16-20 rows. Do not begin shaping the top until you are right at the top of the
thumb. Decrease as for top of hand until 8 stitches remain; finish off.
Make a braid or tassel with the cast-on strands or weave them in on inside.
Wash the mittens. Pull them a little length- and width-wise so that they have the
correct shape and size and then lay them on a handtowel. Press them out with
your hand so that they become smooth and fine.

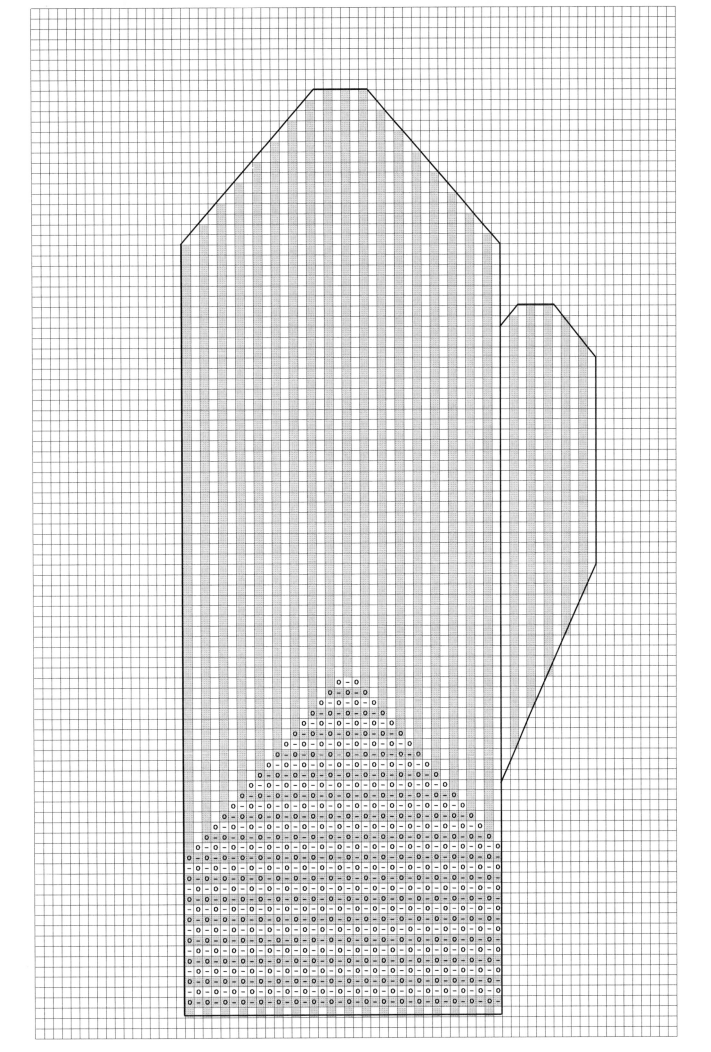

MITTENS   Single Color with a Gusset Thumb and a Wide Cuff

Yarn: 100 grams (3 ½ ounces)
Needles: set of 5 double-pointed needles + an extra needle for gusset stitches, if desired
Notions: A linen or cotton thread for holding thumb stitches

Cuff: cast on 100 stitches and divide them evenly onto 4 needles.
Knit one and a half rows (over 6 needles), a chain path (2 rows) and a knit row.
Decrease the width of the cuff by 4 stitches every 3rd row 7 times until 72 stitches remain.
Decrease rows:
Needles 1 and 3: Knit 10 stitches. Slip 1, knit 1 and pass slip stitch over. Knit the rest of the stitches on the needle.
Needles 2 and 4: Knit until 12 stitches remain on the needle; knit 2 together through front loops and knit the remaining 10 stitches.
Work 5 hook rows to delineate the line between the cuff and the hand. Then knit 1 row and begin the increases for the thumb gusset.
Be sure that the thumbs point in the right direction!

Thumb Gusset:
Increase 1 stitch at each side of the gusset on every other row, placing the thumb just in from the side of the hand, as follows:
Left hand: knit until 4 stitches remain on the needle. Increase in two stitches next to each other and then knit the last 2 stitches.
The next row is worked without increasing. There are now 2 stitches between each increase stitch.
Knit the next row until 6 stitches remain on the needle. Increase in one stitch, knit 2, increase in one stitch and knit the last 2 stitches.
Now there are 4 stitches between each increase. Increase a total of 22 stitches.
Right hand: Knit 2 stitches, increase in the next 2 stitches and knit the last 14 stitches on the needle, etc.
(If there are too many stitches on the "increase" needle, use a sixth needle.)

Hand: Knit 1 row without increasing. Place the 22 stitches which were increased for the thumb onto a waste yarn and cast on 12 new stitches.
Knit 1 row. Return to the stitch count of 72 by forming the 12 cast-on stitches into a little gusset by decreasing 2 stitches every row of the first 6 rows.
Knit 25-30 rows or until the mitten covers the little finger before beginning the top shaping.
Shape with a band decrease until 12 stitches remain; finish off.

Thumb: Place the 22 thumb stitches from the waste yarn onto a needle and knit them. Pick up and knit 14 new stitches where the 12 stitches were cast on at the thumbhole. Use 4 of these 14 stitches for a little gusset by decreasing 2 stitches on each of the first 2 rows. There will be 32 stitches left for the thumb.
Knit 16-20 rows. Do not begin shaping the top until you are right at the top of the thumb. Decrease as for top of hand until 8 stitches remain; finish off, weaving ends on inside.

This mitten could, of course, be knitted with a straight thumb. In that case, knit about 22 rows after the hook rows before you knit in a waste yarn at the thumbhole.

Make a braid or tassel with the cast-on strands or weave them in on inside.

Wash the mittens. Pull them a little length- and width-wise so that they have the correct shape and size and lay them on a handtowel. Press them out with your hand so that they become smooth and fine.

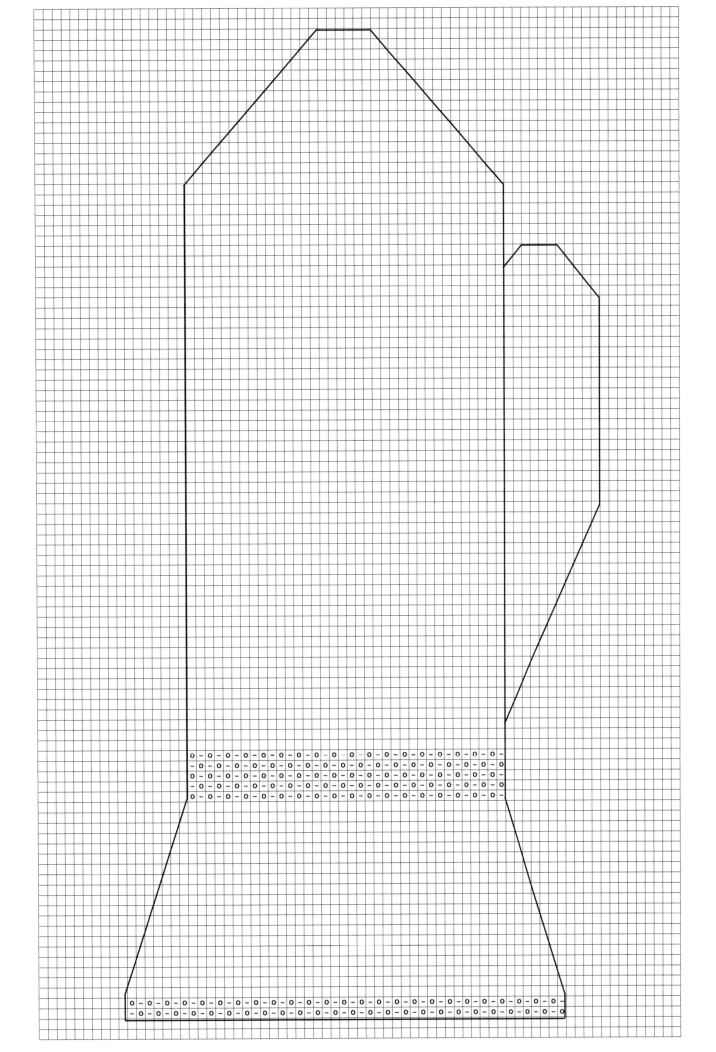

STOCKINGS

Yarn: 3 x 100 grams (approximately 11 ounces)
Needles: Set of 5 double-pointed needles
Notions: A linen or cotton waste yarn to set aside the foot stitches

Leg

Cast on 128 stitches (about 35.5 cm/14 inches around at the calf). Divide stitches so that there are 32 stitches on each needle. Knit one and a half rows so that the tassel will be at the outside and the row changes at the inside of the leg.
Work a patterned cuff over about 25 rows without any decreasing. Knit a whole row and begin decreasing at the *center back* on every 3rd row until you have 84 stitches remaining.
The decreases can be worked at each side of a deep purl "seam" which is made by purling 2 stitches one after the other, working each with both strands at the same time.
Work until 5 stitches remain at the center back: Make a decrease through front loops. Knit 2 stitches; purl 2 stitches, each with both strands at the same time. Knit 2 more stitches. Make a decrease through back loops.

If you want a pattern which looks like the gusset at the side of the calf on sewn stockings, plan ahead and place it at the desired height on the leg.

Continue working without decreasing but continue making the "seam" and gusset. Try it on to be sure it is long enough.

Heel

If you knit the heel before the foot, you can later try the sock on to be sure the foot is long enough. Begin by checking that the same number of stitches is on each needle.
Set aside the stitches for the *instep* onto a strong waste yarn. From that yarn, you can pick up new stitches between the old stitches. Knit these stitches with the sock yarn. Straighten the set-in strand. (You can also knit in a waste yarn in the same way as you do when you make the thumbhole for a straight thumb.)
Knit one more row and then begin to decrease with, for example, a band decrease. Decrease 2 stitches at each side on every row.
Finish off the heel when 24 stitches remain.

Foot

Draw out the waste yarn holding the instep stitches (or remove the knitted-in waste yarn).
At the same time, at one side of the opening, pick up and knit stitches. On the other side, pick up and knit stitches from the loops. There should be 84 stitches for the foot. If you think the foot looks too wide, you can decrease 1 stitch at each side every other row a few times.
Don't begin shaping the toe until you are at the tip of the little toe. Decrease 2 stitches at each side every other row 2 times. Then decrease on every row until 28 stitches remain. Finish off.

Because you have knitted the heel and foot "separately," it is easy to repair a torn stocking. If the hole is on the heel, cut it off and knit a new heel. If the hole is somewhere on the foot cut away at the bad part and knit to the end of the sock.

If you want to knit a pair of socks with a short leg, cast on 84 stitches and knit the leg. The heel and foot are knitted following the instructions above.

Unfortunately, two-end knitted stockings don't stay up on their own. Formerly, stocking bands had to be knitted to hold up the stockings. I think stockings are lovely even if they do slip down.

CAP   Skullcap

Yarn: 100 grams (3 ½ ounces) total
Needles: 40 cm/16 inch circular needle and double-pointed needles

When you are knitting caps, you need to keep in mind that two-end knitting stretches out rather a lot. This cap measured 53 cm/21 inches when newly knitted and unwashed. After being used for a year and a couple of washes, it now measures 58 cm/23 inches.

Cast on 192 stitches. Use cast-on method 2 to stabilize the edging as much as possible.
Begin by working a row with only knit stitches.
Then work a pattern (a pattern repeat of 4, 6, 8, 12, 16, or 24 stitches is recommended) over 35-40 rows, depending on how high you want the cap to be.

Decrease with the method of your choice until 16 stitches remain. The spacing of the decreases can be varied, depending on how conical or round you want the top to be.
If you decrease one stitch at 16 places or two stitches at 8 places evenly divided over the row, on every 3rd row, your cap will have a more conical shape. If you work the decreases as above only 4-5 times and then decrease every other row, the shape will be rounder.
If you are knitting a striped pattern, it is easiest to maintain the stripe pattern if you double decrease at 8 places around the row.
Change to double-pointed needles when there are too few stitches to fit on the circular needle.

Cut yarn. Thread through remaining stitches, pull tight, and weave in ends on wrong side.

Wash the cap and smooth it out. Look through your cupboards and closets to find a ball, vase, pot, or some object with the same shape as a head so that you can dry your cap on it.

CAP

Yarn: 100 grams (3 ½ ounces)
Needles: 40 cm/16 inch circular needle and double-pointed needles
Notions: 2 small markers

Cast on 192 stitches.
Work a pattern over approximately 50 rows.
Place a marker at each side so that you can easily see where to decrease.
Decrease 2 stitches on each side every row until 4 stitches remain. When
there are too few stitches to go around the circular needle, shift stitches to
double-pointed needles. Cut yarn, draw through remaining stitches and pull
tight.

Fasten a pompon to the top or make a cord or braid to hang a tassel from.
For a fuller cord than one using only the cut yarns, sew in an extra piece of
yarn. Make a cord or braid about 5 cm/2" long and knot a tassel into the end.

CAP   Pillbox

Yarn: a little more than 100 grams (3 ½ ounces)
Needles: 7 double-pointed needles and a 60 cm/24" circular needle size 2.5 mm/US 1.5

The advantage of this design is that it doesn't stretch.

Begin by knitting the band around the head. It is knitted as a long tube so that the entire band is doubled.
Cast on 80 stitches with cast-on method 1 which is easy to pull out. Divide the stitches evenly onto 4 needles.
Knit in the round for 180 rows or to a length which will go around the head (about 60 cm/24"). To make it easier to pick up the stitches for the top of the cap, purl 1 on one edge of the tube.

Remove the cast-on thread and weave together the ends of the tube.
Pick up and knit 1 stitch from each row (= 180 stitches) around one edge of the tube by inserting the circular needle into the loops of the purl stitches. Work the first row through these loops and divide the stitches onto 6 double-pointed needles.

On every row, decrease 6 stitches evenly around the row until 12 stitches remain. After several decrease rows, you can continue with only 4 double-pointed needles.

If you are knitting a striped pattern, remember to twist the correct color forward.

Cut yarns and thread them through the remaining stitches; weave ends in on wrong side.

Wash the cap and block it on an upturned straight-sided bucket or something similar so that the cap will be shaped correctly.

FINISHING and GARMENT CARE

Washing

After a garment has been knitted, it needs to be washed even if the yarn was washed before knitting. Actually, a garment can become rather dirty during the process of knitting. In addition, a garment needs to be moistened after knitting so that the fibers in the yarn will align correctly.

Three factors need to be taken into consideration when washing a wool garment in order to avoid shrinkage or felting. The heat of the water, agitation, and washing soap all influence the fibers' propensity to felt. If all three factors are present at the same time, the risk of felting is great. If only two of the factors are present, the risk is somewhat diminished. If only one factor is present, the risk that something will happen is most unlikely. Time also has a certain influence. If one leaves a wool garment agitating in cold water for a very long time it will eventually felt.

I work in the following way when I wash wool garments *by hand*:

I press the garment down into warm water with wool wash, color-free dishwashing liquid, or shampoo added and squeeze it very carefully. With this method, all three factors for felting are present. The warm water and washing liquid are necessary, so the agitation has to be very careful. Let the garment lie in the warm water for only 5 minutes. In the first rinse, the water temperature will have lowered a little and, at the same time, there should not be much soap left. The effect of two of the factors has been lessened and so now the garment can tolerate a little more elbow grease to get rid of smudges or very dirty parts.

Rinse the garment two times in a sink, lowering the temperature slightly with each rinse. After this, two of the felting factors have almost totally gone away. The temperature is low and there is almost no soap left. Agitation alone will not hurt the garment so I do the last rinse in the washing machine with cold water (with a small amount of white vinegar added if you want to add luster).

Finally, I centrifuge the garment in order to get as much water out as possible. If you have a centrifuge with a very high spin, be sure and turn it off before it is up to full speed. Wool can retain so much water that a large two-end knitted garment is next to impossible to handle if you don't centrifuge it a little. This works well without harming the garment because the first two factors (warm water and soap) are no longer present. The old rule about wringing out wool garments in a towel persists from the time when we didn't have access to centrifuges and were forced to remove the water in some other way.

Modern front-loading washing machines have wool programs which are quite reliable. The first machines with wool programs were suitable only for super-wash garments because they had a strong agitation during the wash cycle. Test your machine before you put in a valuable wool garment. The machine should agitate with only small movements during the wash, swing carefully and turn completely only once in a while. Because all three risk factors are present during the wash cycle, the movement must be minimal. The first rinse cycle should also be careful. When two of the risk factors are gone then the machine can continue with normal rinsing and centrifuging.

After washing, I lay the garment out on a Turkish towel on the floor or on a table and block it out the correct form. Then I pound it with my fists and press it hard with my palms over the whole garment so that it is flat and fine. You only need to work on one side because you will press it hard enough that the underneath side will also be flat. Draw in the edges a little bit and work them extra so that they don't roll up eventually. A light weight can be laid over long edges or they can be pinned during drying.

I hang skirts for drying after they have been smoothed by pounding with the fists on a flat surface. You will get little "wings" if they lie flat to dry.

When the garment is dry for a little while, it is ready to be worn.

Fulling, Felting, and Shrinking

We have several different terms for handling and manipulating wool and wool fabrics. Woolen goods can be fulled or felted to effectively bring out the most positive qualities of wool fibers while minimizing the negative qualities. Shrinking is done by mistake.

Wool is not only warm; it also has unique and good water absorption and water dispersal powers while at the same time, it is water repellent. Damp wool warms when it becomes wet in contrast to all other fibers. The one negative quality of wool is that it doesn't stand up well to wear and tear. When a finished garment is fulled, there are then more fibers per square cm/inch so the fabric wears better. For that reason, the denser a garment is, the more wind resistant.

When one fulls or felts a garment, it also shrinks. Before making a garment, you need to consider how much fulling it will have afterwards. The maximum fulling for a garment can be up to 50%, depending on how the yarn was spun and what type of wool was spun for the yarn.

When fulling a garment, you do what you shouldn't when simply washing a garment. You manipulate the piece aggressively in warm water with detergent. For fulling, you can use soap, colorless dish washing liquid or hard water detergent. With small pieces, such as mittens and caps, you can work as you do when felting wool. Dampen the garment in warm water and put it on a counter and knead it. Immerse it in the warm water again. For a larger garment, use a washing or felting board to scrub against. At first, it will seem limp and difficult but, when you've worked the fabric a while, it will start to full. The fabric will begin to feel more stable and manageable. Then you need to watch carefully so that the garment isn't fulled too much. If you want to shrink the fabric most in length, then scrub it lengthwise or work it across the width if you want more shrinkage there.

If, when the garment has dried, you think that the piece hasn't been fulled enough, just wet it again and repeat the fulling process. If you have fulled it too much, I can only sympathize!

Garment Care

It is worth the time to take good care of a valuable garment. Woolen garments don't need to be washed as often as those made of synthetics which should be washed after every wearing. It should be enough to wash a wool garment only a few times a season. However, you should air the piece often. Shake off, brush, and pick off flecks. Airing out is best in humid weather. Wool retains all of its good qualities even when it is dirty in a way which no other man-made fiber can.

Remember that most hand knitting yarns are not moth-proofed. Both wool yarns and garments must be aired out every now and again so that they won't become moth food. Do not let a pile of woolens lie undisturbed. Shifting the pile now and then minimizes the risk of moth infestation because moths are happiest at the bottom of an undisturbed pile.

Should you have the misfortune of a moth infestation, it helps to have access to a sauna or steamroom. Leaving the woolens in a very warm sauna for a while will kill the eggs, larvae, and moths. This will also work in the freezer if you repeat the process several times.

TIPS

It is easy to splice wool yarns!
Neaten both yarn ends so the finished join is not too lumpy.
Open the ply on each yarn end and pull off about an inch of a single strand from each end. Overlap the ends and spit on them gently. Aggressively roll the ends together with your palms, almost until the yarn "burns" in your hands. Then the fibers will have felted together and the join will be stronger than the yarn.

If you want to be certain that the pieces being knitted will all be the same length, you must count the number of rows. Measuring with a measuring tape can give you the wrong results. The piece which you pull and adjust for trying on as you work can stretch out a bit. The piece which was knitted without being pulled on will have snug and unstretched fibers. If you measure these pieces against each other, the last knitted one will be too short.
It is usually easiest to count rows on the wrong side in two-end knitting.

Knit both mittens or socks at the same time, so you won't forget what you did as you knitted.

When you knit or add in a supplementary thread (on, for example, the thumbhole or a sock heel or when you are setting aside the stitches for the sleeve of a sweater), use linen or cotton thread. Wool yarn can fuzz up and leave a streak of color.

Two-end knitting can stretch rather a lot across the width and almost not at all in length. That's why a cap with a turned-up edge can become too wide. Different yarns stretch in varying degrees.

Two-end knitting tolerates wear a little better than regular knitting because it is tighter. There are more fibers per square centimeter/inch to wear through before a hole appears.

Most newly-knitted garments pill. Wool garments pill until the shorter fibers have disappeared. Garments made of synthetic fibers do not stop pilling until there is nothing left.

I've often been asked if it doesn't take a really long time to two-end knit. Yes, certainly, it takes longer to work stockinette in two-end knitting than in regular knitting. However, there are many patterns in regular knitting which take much more time and trouble than pattern-knitting in two-end knitting.

No one knits too tightly in two-end knitting but I have sometimes seen it too loosely knitted. If you know that you knit too loosely, keep in mind that the gauge depends on how hard you pull when you pick up the strand with the index finger in order to knit the next stitch. You can draw in the last-knitted stitch as hard as you want without the knitting becoming more compact.

Don't pull the strands for all they're worth when you change double-pointed needles. When you knit on double-pointed needles, go easy so that there is a tiny gap between the needles. You will be tempted to pull the strands so that it will look more even. The harder you pull, the bigger the gap!

When I say that a thing should be done in the "wrong direction" or in the "wrong way," I put it in quotes because I actually think that seldom can something be done in the "wrong way." It is, for example, a mistake to bring the yarn down over the needle, but try it in two-end knitting with an

S-plied yarn. It is "wrong" but the result looks quite good.

Damp wool is warming. If you have a cat at home, it won't be long before it is sleeping happily on a wet wool garment.

I usually follow the old pattern knitting tradition of not being too fussy about a pattern repeat meeting at the end of a row. When the row is completed, I begin the next on the first stitch of the pattern repeat. I place the row changes so that it is less visible. If the seam doesn't work to hide it, then I prefer to bring it out with a border rather than changing the stitch count. The main thing is to think about how to place the pattern when you begin the piece that that it looks as fine as possible where it is most visible.

If you want to design your own patterns but have difficulty hatching ideas, it is worthwhile leafing through old cross-stitch patterns, weaving books, and other pattern books. Various textile techniques have always lent ideas to others.

Two-end knitting makes a wonderful ground for embroidery. In the past, it was common to embroider color designs on both men's and women's mittens.

Give the remains of yarn skeins and hopelessly worn-out wool garments back to the worms in the earth. Put them under a bush and cover them with a bit of soil or grass clippings so that it won't look messy. Berries and other ornamental bushes will get some nourishment from your scraps for a long time. [translator's note: in Swedish the word for worm is "mask" and for stitch "maska" so giving your leftover "stitches" to the worms is quite appropriate!]

BIBLIOGRAPHY AND SOURCES

Dandanell, Brigitta and Ulla Danielsson. <u>Tvåändsstickat</u>. Falun and
    Stockholm, Sweden: Dalarna's Museum and LTs Förlag, 1984.
    IBSN 91-36-01928-3. English translation by Robin Orm Hansen.
    <u>Twined Knitting: A Swedish Folkcraft Technique</u>. Loveland,
    Colorado: Interweave Press, 1989. IBSN 1-883010-02-0.

Dandanell, Birgitta and Kerstin Gustafsson. <u>Studieplan i tvåändsstickning</u>
    [Study Plan for Two-End Knitting]. Medborgarskolan and Dalarna's
    Museum, 1981. 2nd edition, 1984. Bokmalen, Medborgarskolans
    förlag.

Frederiksen, Tove. <u>Tvebindning</u> [Two-End Knitting]. Copenhagen,
    Denmark, 1982. ISBN 87-04064-5.

Frisk, Gun. <u>Tvåändsstickat. Nya Modeller</u> [Two-End Knitting: New
    Designs]. Booklet published by Dalarna's Hemslöjd [Handicrafts],
    Falun, Sweden.

Gunnars, Anita. <u>Vantar mössor sockor & sjalar</u> [Mittens, Caps, Socks, and
    Shawls]. Västerås, Sweden: ICA Bokförlag, 2001.
    ISBN 91-534-2074-8

Gustafsson, Kerstin. <u>Gamla textila tekniker i ull</u> [Old Textile Techniques in
    Wool]. Stockholm, Sweden: LTs förlag, 1988. ISBN 91-36-02703-0

_____: <u>Textila tekniker med speciell anknytning till ull</u> [Textile
    Techniques with Special Connections to Wool]. Booklet published
    by Kerstin Gustafsson.

Gustafsson, Kerstin and Allan Waller. <u>ULL Hemligheter, möjligheter, fär-
    digheter</u> [WOOL: Secrets, Possibilities, Skills]. LTs förlag, 1987.
    ISBN 91-36-02519-4.

Westman, Berit. <u>Tvåändsstickning</u>. Västmanlands Läns Hemslöjdsförening,
    Västerås.

<u>Tvåändsstickning, arbetsbeskrivning</u> [Two-End Knitting: Instructions].
    Dalarnas hemslöjd and Dalarna's Museum, Falun.

Walker, Barbara G. <u>Mosaic Knitting</u>. Cary Bluff, Wisconsin: Schoolhouse
    Press. ISBN 0-942018-15-X